The Orbis Pictus of John Amos Comenius

The Educational Classic – The First Illustrated Children's Textbook, Published in 1658

By John Amos Comenius

Published by Pantianos Classics

ISBN-13: 978-1-78987-394-8

First published in 1658

This translation to English was first published in 1887 and is based on a reprint dated to 1728

Contents

It may not be generally known that Comenius was once solicited to become President of Harvard College. The following is a quotation from Vol. II, p. 14, of Cotton Mather's Magnalia:

"That brave old man, Johannes Amos Commenius, the fame of whose worth has been trumpetted as far as more than three languages (whereof everyone is indebted unto his Janua) could carry it, was indeed agreed withal, by one Mr. Winthrop in his travels through the low countries, to come over to New England, and illuminate their Colledge and country, in the quality of a President, which was now become vacant. But the solicitations of the Swedish Ambassador diverting him another way, that incomparable Moravian became not an American."

This was on the resignation of President Dunster, in 1654 — Note of Prof. Payne, Compayre's History of Education, Boston, 1886, p. 125.

Editor's Preface

When it is remembered that this work is not only an educational classic of prime importance, but that it was the first picture-book ever made for children and was for a century the most popular text-book in Europe, and yet has been for many years unattainable on account of its rarity, the wonder is, not that it is reproduced now but that it has not been reproduced before. But the difficulty has been to find a satisfactory copy. Many as have been the editions, few copies have been preserved. It was a book children were fond of and wore out in turning the leaves over and over to see the pictures. Then as the old copper-plates became indistinct they were replaced by wood-engravings, of coarse execution, and often of changed treatment. Von Raumer complains that the edition of 1755 substitutes for the original cut of the Soul, (No. 43, as here given,) a picture of an eye, and in a table the figures 1. I. II. 1. I. II, and adds that it is difficult to recognize in this an expressive psychological symbol, and to explain it. In an edition I have, published in Vienna in 1779, this cut is omitted altogether, and indeed there are but 82 in place of the 157 found in earlier editions, the following, as numbered in this edition, being omitted:

1, the alphabet, 2, 36, 43, 45, 66, 68, 75, 76, 78-80, 87, 88, 92-122, 124, 126, 128, 130-141.

On the other hand, the Vienna edition contains a curious additional cut. It gives No. 4, the Heaven, practically as in this edition, but puts another cut under it in which the earth is revolving about the sun; and after the statement of Comenius, *"Coelum rotator, et ambit terram, in medio stantem"* interpolates: "prout veteres crediderunt; recentiores enim defendunt motum terrae circa solem" [as the ancients used to think; for later authorities hold that the motion of the earth is about the sun.]

Two specimen pages from another edition are inserted in Payne's Compayré's History of Education (between pp. 126, 127). The cut is the representative of No. 103 in this edition, but those who compare them will see not only how much coarser is the execution of the wood-cut Prof. Payne has copied, but what liberties have been taken with the design. The only change in the Latin text, however, is from *Designat Figuras rerum* in the original, to *Figuram rerum designat.*

In this edition the cuts are unusually clear copies of the copper-plates of the first edition of 1658, from which we have also taken the Latin text. The text. for the English translation is from the English edition of 1727, in which for the first time the English words were so arranged as to stand opposite their Latin equivalents.

The cuts have been reproduced with great care by the photographic process. I thought best not to permit them to be retouched, preferring occasional indistinctness to modern tampering with the originals that would make them less authentic.

The English text is unchanged from that of the 1727 edition, except in rare instances where substitutions have been made for single words not now permissible. The typography suggests rather than imitates the quaintness of the original, and the paper was carefully selected to produce so far as practicable the impression of the old hand-presses.

In short my aim has been to put within the reach of teachers at a moderate price a satisfactory reproduction of this important book; and if the sale of the *Orbis Pictus* seems to warrant it, I hope subsequently to print as a companion volume the *Vestibulum* and *Janua* of the same author, of which I have choice copies.

C. W. Bardeen.

Syracuse, Sept. 28, 1887.

Comments upon the Orbis Pictus

During four years he here prosecuted his efforts in behalf of education with commendable success, and wrote, among other works, his celebrated Orbis Pictus, which has passed through a great many editions,, and survived a multitude of imitations. — Smith's History of Education, N. Y, 1842, p. 129.

The most eminent educator of the seventeenth century, however, was John Amos Comenius His Orbis Sensualium Pictus, published in 1657, enjoyed a still higher renown. The text was much the same with the Janua, being intended as a kind of elementary encyclopaedia; but *it differed from all previous text-books,* in being illustrated with pictures, on copper and wood, of the various topics discussed in it. This book was universally popular. In those portions of Germany where the schools had been broken up by the "Thirty years' war," mothers taught their children from its pages. Corrected and amended by later editors, it continued for nearly two hundred years, to be a text-book of the German schools. — History and Progress of Education, by Philobiblius, N. Y, 1860, p. 210.

The "Janua" would, therefore, have had but a short-lived popularity with teachers, and a still shorter with learners, if Comenius had not carried out his principle of appealing to the senses, and called in the artist. The result was the "Orbis Pictus," a book which proved a favorite with young and old, and maintained its ground in many a school for more than a century...I am sorry I cannot give a specimen of this celebrated book with its quaint pictures. The artist, of course, was wanting in the technical skill which is now commonly displayed even in the cheapest publications, but this renders his delineations none the less entertaining. As a picture of the life and manners of the seventeenth century, the work has great historical interest, which will, I hope, secure for it another English edition. — Quick's Educational Reformers, 1868; Syracuse edition, p. 79.

But the principle on which he most insisted is that the teaching of words and things must go together, hand in hand. When we consider how much time is spent over new languages, what waste of energy is lavished on mere preparation, how it takes so long to lay a foundation that there is no time to lay a building upon it, we must conclude that it is in the acceptance and development of this principle that the improvement of education will in the future consist. Any one who attempts to inculcate this great reform will find that its first principles are contained in the writings of Comenius. — Encyclopaedia Britannica, 9th edition, vii. 674.

The first edition of this celebrated book was published at Nuremberg in 1657; soon after a translation was made into English by Charles Hoole. The last English edition appeared in 1777, and this was reprinted in America in 18 12. This was the first illustrated school-book, and was the first attempt at what now passes under the name of "object lessons." — Short History of Education, W. H. Payne, Syracuse, 1881, p. 103.

Of these, the "Janua" and the "Orbis" were translated into most European and some of the Oriental languages. It is evident that these practices of Comenius contain the germs of things afterwards connected with the names of Pestalozzi and Stow. It also may be safely assumed that many methods that are now in practical use, were then not unknown to earliest teachers. — Gill's Systems of Education, London, 1876, p. 13.

The more we reflect on the method of Comenius, the more we shall see it is replete with suggestiveness, and we shall feel surprised that so much wisdom can have lain in the path of schoolmasters for two hundred and fifty years, and that they have never stooped to avail themselves of its treasures. — Browning's Introduction to the History of Educational Theories, 1882, New York edition, p. 67.

The "Orbis Pictus," the first practical application of the intuitive method, had an extraordinary success, and has served as a model for the innumerable illustrated books which for three centuries have invaded the schools. — Compayre's History of Pedagogy, Payne's translation, Boston, 1886, p. 127.

He remained at Patak four years, which were characterized by surprising literary activity. During this short period he produced no less than fifteen different works, among them his "World Illustrated" (*Orbis Pictus*), the most famous of all his writings. It admirably applied the principle that words and things should be learned together...The "World Illustrated" had an enormous circulation, and remained for a long time the most popular text-book in Europe. — Painter's History of Education, N.Y, 1886, p. 206.

Or, si ce livre n'est qu'un equivalent le la véritable intuition; si, ensuite, le contenu du tout paraît fort defectueux, au point de vue de la science de nos jours; si, enfin, un effort exagéré pour l'integrité de la conception de l'enfant a créé, pour les choses modernes, trop de dénominations latines qui paraissent douteuses, l'*Orbis pictus* etait pourtant, pour son temps, une oeuvre très originale et très spirituelle, qui fit faire un grand progrès a la pedagogie et servit longtemps de livre d'ecole utile et de modèle á d'innomorables livres d'images, souvent pires. — Historie D'Éducation, Frederick Dittes, Redolfi's French translation, Paris, 1880, p. 178.

Here Comenius wrote, among others, his second celebrated work the "Orbis Pictus." He was not, however, able to finish it in Hungary for want of a skilful engraver on copper. For such a one he carried it to Michael Endter, the bookseller at Nuremberg, but the engraving delayed the publication of the book for three years more. In 1657 Comenius expressed the hope that it would appear during the next autumn. With what great approbation the work was received at its first appearance, is shown by the fact that within two years, in 1659, Endter had published a second enlarged edition. — Karl Von Raumer, translated in Barnard's Journal of Education, v. 260.

The "Janua" had an enormous sale, and was published in many languages, but the editions and sale of the "Orbis Pictus" far exceeded those of the "Janua," and, indeed, for some time it was the most popular text-book in Europe, and deservedly so. — Laurie's John Amos Comenius, Boston edition, p. 185.

JOH. AMOS COMENII

Orbis Sensualium Pictus:

HOC EST

Omnium principalium in Mundo Rerum, & in Vita Actionum,

PICTURA & NOMENCLATURA.

JOH. AMOS COMENIUS'S

VISIBLE WORLD:

OR, A

Nomenclature, and Pictures

OF ALL THE

CHIEF THINGS that are in the WORLD, and of MENS EMPLOYMENTS therein;

In above 150 COPPER CUTS.

WRITTEN

By the Author in Latin and High Dutch, being one of his last ESSAYS; and the most suitable to Childrens Capacity of any he hath hitherto made.

Translated into English

By CHARLES HOOLE, M. A.

For the Use of Young Latin Scholars.

The ELEVENTH EDITION Corrected, and the English made to answer Word for Word to the Latin.

Nihil est in intellectu, quod non prius fuit in sensu. Arist.

London; Printed for, and sold by *John* and *Benj. Sprint*, at the *Bell* in *Little Britain*, 1728.

Gen. ii. 19, 20.

The Lord God brought unto *Adam* every Beast of the Field, and every Fowl of the Air, to see what he would call them. And *Adam* gave Names to all Cattle, and to the Fowl of the Air, and to every Beast of the Field.

Gen. ii. 19, 20.

Adduxit Dominus Deus ad Adam *cuncta Animantia Terrae & universa volatilia Coeli ut videret quomodo vocaret illa. Appellavitque* Adam *Nominibus suis cuncta Animantia, & universa volatilia Coeli, & omnes Bestias Agri.*

1. A. Comenii opera Didactica par. 1. p. 6, Amst. 1657. fol.

Didacticae nostrae prora & puppis esto: Investigare, & invenire modum, quo Docentes minus doceant, Discentes vero plus discant: Scholae minus habeant Strepitus, nauseae, vani laboris; plus autem otii, deliciarum, solidique profectus: Respublica Christiana minus tenebrarum confusionis dissidiorum; plus lucis, ordinis, pacis & tranquilitatis.

The Author's Preface to the Reader

I*nstruction is the means to expel Rudeness,* with which young wits ought to be well furnished in Schools: But so, as that the teaching be 1. True, 2. Full, 3. Clear, and 4. Solid.

1. It will be *true,* if nothing be taught but such as is beneficial to one's life; lest there be a cause of complaining afterwards. We know not necessary things, because we have not learned things necessary.

2. It will be *full,* if the mind be polished for wisdom, the tongue for eloquence, and the hands for a neat way of living. This will be that *grace* of one's life, *to be wise, to act, to speak.*

3. 4. It will be *clear,* and by that, firm and *solid,* if whatever is taught and learned, be not obscure, or confused, but apparent, distinct, and articulate, as the fingers on the hands.

The ground of this business, is, that sensual objects may be rightly presented to the senses, for fear they may not be received. I say, and say it again aloud, that this last is the foundation of all the rest: because we can neither act nor speak wisely, unless we first rightly understand all the things which are to be done, and whereof we are to speak. Now there is nothing in the understanding, which was not before in the sense. And therefore to exercise the senses well about the right perceiving the differences of things, will be to lay the grounds for all wisdom, and all wise discourse, and all discreet actions in one's course of life. Which, because it is commonly neglected in schools, and the things which are to be learned are offered to scholars, without being understood or being rightly presented to the senses, it cometh to pass, that the work of teaching and learning goeth heavily onward, and affordeth little benefit.

See here then a new help for schools, A Picture and Nomenclature of all the chief things in the world, and of men's actions in their way of living: Which, that you, good Masters, may not be loath to run over with your scholars, I will tell you, in short, what good you may expect from it.

It is *a little Book*, as you see, of no great bulk, yet a brief of the whole world, and a whole language: full of Pictures, Nomenclatures, and Descriptions of things.

1. *The Pictures* are the representation of all visible things, (to which also things invisible are reduced after their fashion) of the whole world. And that in that very order of things, in which they are described in the *Janua Latinae Linguae;* and with that fulness, that nothing very necessary or of great concernment is omitted.

II. *The Nomenclatures* are the Inscriptions, or Titles set every one over their own Pictures, expressing the whole thing by its own general term.

III. *The Descriptions* are the explications of the parts of the Picture, so expressed by their own proper terms, as that same figure which is added to every piece of the picture, and the term of it, always sheweth what things belongeth one to another.

Which such Book, and in such a dress may (I hope) serve.

1. To entice witty children to it, that they may not conceit a torment to be in the school, but dainty fare. For it is apparent, that children (even from their infancy almost) are delighted with Pictures, and willingly please their eyes with these lights: And it will be very well worth the pains to have once brought it to pass, that scare-crows may be taken away out of Wisdom's Gardens.

II. This same little Book will serve to stir up the Attention, which is to be fastened upon things, and even to be sharpened more and more: which is also a great matter. For the Senses (being the main guides of childhood, because therein the mind doth not as yet raise up itself to an abstracted contemplation of things) evermore seek their own objects, and if they be away, they grow dull, and wry themselves hither and thither out of a weariness of themselves: but when their objects are present, they grow merry, wax lively, and willingly suffer themselves to be fastened upon them, till the thing be sufficiently discerned. This Book then will do a good piece of service in taking (especially flickering) wits, and preparing them for deeper studies.

III. Whence a third good will follow; that children being won hereunto, and drawn over with this way of heeding, may be furnished with the knowledge of the prime things that are in the world, by sport and merry pastime. In a word, this Book will serve for the more pleasing using of the *Vestibulum* and

Janua Linguarum, for which end it was even at the first chiefly intended. Yet if it like any, that it be bound up in their native tongues also, it promiseth three good thing of itself.

1. First it will afford a device for learning to read more easily than hitherto, especially having a symbolical alphabet set before it, to wit, the characters of the several letters, with the image of that creature, whose voice that letter goeth about to imitate, pictur'd by it. For the young *Abc* scholar will easily remember the force of every character by the very looking upon the creature, till the imagination being strengthened by use, can readily afford all things; and then having looked over *a table of the chief syllables* also (which yet was not thought necessary to be added to this book) he may proceed to the viewing of the Pictures, and the inscriptions set over 'em. Where again the very looking upon the thing pictured suggesting the name of the thing, will tell him how the title of the picture is to be read. And thus the whole book being gone over by the bare titles of the pictures, reading cannot but be learned; and indeed too, which thing is to be noted, without using any ordinary tedious spelling, that most troublesome torture of wits, which may wholly be avoided by this method. For the often reading over the Book, by those larger descriptions of things, and which are set after the Pictures, will be able perfectly to beget a habit of reading.

II. The same book being used in English, in English Schools, will serve for the perfect learning of the whole English tongue, and that from the bottom; because by the aforesaid descriptions of things, the words and phrases of the whole language are found set orderly in their own places. And a short English Grammar might be added at the end, clearly resolving the speech already understood into its parts; shewing the declining of the several words, and reducing those that are joined together under certain rules.

III. Thence a new benefit cometh, that that very English Translation may serve for the more ready and pleasant learning of the Latin tongue: as one may see in this Edition, the whole book being so translated, that every where one word answereth to the word over against it, and the book is in all things the same, only in two idioms, as a man clad in a double garment. And there might be also some observations and advertisements added in the end, touching those things only, wherein the use of the Latin tongue differeth from the English. For where there is no difference, there needeth no advertisement to be given. But, because the *first tasks of learners ought to be little and single,* we have filled this first book of training one up to see a thing of himself, with nothing but rudiments, that is, with the chief of things and words, or with the grounds of the whole world, and the whole language, and of all our understanding about things. If a more perfect description of things, and a fuller knowledge of a language, and a clearer light of the understanding be sought after (as they ought to be) they are to be found somewhere whither there will now be an easy passage by this our little Encyclopoedia of things subject to the senses. Something remaineth to be said touching the more cheerful use of this book.

1. Let it be given to children into their hands to delight themselves withal as they please, with the sight of the pictures, and making them as familiar to themselves as may be, and that even at home before they be put to school.

II. Then let them be examined ever and anon (especially now in the school) what this thing or that thing is, and is called, so that they may see nothing which they know not how to name, and that they can name nothing which they cannot shew.

III. And let the things named them be shewed, not only in the Picture, but also in themselves; for example, the parts of the body, clothes, books, the house, utensils, &c.

IV. Let them be suffered also to imitate the Pictures by hand, if they will, nay rather, let them be encouraged, that they may be willing: first, thus to quicken the attention also towards the things; and to observe the proportion of the parts one towards another; and lastly to practise the nimbleness of the hand, which is good for many things.

V. If anything here mentioned, cannot be presented to the eye, it will be to no purpose at all to offer them by themselves to the scholars; as colours, relishes, &c, which cannot here be pictured out with ink. For which reason it were to be wished, that things rare and not easy to be met withal at home, might be kept ready in every great school, that they may be shewed also, as often as any words are to be made of them, to the scholars.

Thus at last this school would indeed become a school of things obvious to the senses, and an entrance to the school intellectual. But enough: Let us come to the thing it self.

The Translator, to all judicious and Industrious School-Masters

-----

Gentlemen.

There are a few of you (I think) but have seen, and with great willingness made use of (or at least perused) many of the Books of this well-deserving Author Mr. John Comenius, which for their profitableness to the speedy attainment of a language, have been translated in several countries, out of Latin into their own native tongue.

Now the general verdict (after trial made) that hath passed, touching those formerly extant, is this, that they are indeed of singular use, and very advantageous to those of more discretion, (especially to such as already have a smattering of Latin) to help their memories to retain what they have scatteringly gotten here and there, to furnish them with many words, which (perhaps) they had not formerly read, or so well observed; but to young children (whom we have chiefly to instruct) as those that are ignorant altogether of things and words, and prove rather a meer toil and burthen, than a delight and furtherance.

For to pack up many words in memory, of things not conceived in the mind, is to fill the head with empty imaginations, and to make the learner more to admire the multitude and variety (and thereby, to become discouraged,) than to care to treasure them up, in hopes to gain more knowledge of what they mean.

He hath therefore in some of his latter works seemed to move retrograde, and striven to come nearer the reach of tender wits: and in this present Book, he hath, according to my judgment, descended to the very bottom of what is to be taught, and proceeded (as nature it self doth) in an orderly way; first to exercise the senses well, by representing their objects to them, and then to fasten upon the intellect by impressing the first notions of things upon it, and linking them on to another by a rational discourse. Whereas indeed, we, generally missing this way, do teach children as we do parrots, to speak they know not what, nay which is worse, we, taking the way of teaching little ones by Grammar only at the first, do puzzle their imaginations with abstractive terms and secondary intentions, which till they be somewhat acquainted with things, and the words belonging to them, in the language which they learn, they cannot apprehend what they mean. And this I guess to be the reason, why many great persons do resolve sometimes not to put a child to school till he be at least eleven or twelve years of age, presuming that he having then taken notice of most things, will sooner get the knowledge of the words which are applied to them in any language. But the gross misdemeanor of such children for the most part, have taught many parents to be hasty enough to send their own to school, if not that they may learn, yet (at least) that they might be kept out of harm's way; and yet if they do not profit for the time they have been at school, (no respect at all being had for their years) the Master shall be sure enough to bear the blame.

So that a School-master had need to bend his wits to come within the compass of a child's capacity of six or seven years of age (seeing we have now such commonly brought to our Grammar-schools to learn the Latin Tongue) and to make that they may learn with as much delight and willingness, as himself would teach with dexterity and ease. And at present I know no better help to forward his young scholars than this little Book, which was for this purpose contrived by the Author in the German and Latin Tongues.

What profitable use may be had thereof, respecting chiefly that his own country and language, he himself hath told you in his preface; but what use we may here make of it in our Grammar-schools, as it is now translated into English, I shall partly declare; leaving all other men, according to my wont, to their own discretion and liberty, to use or refuse it, as they please. So soon then as a child can read English perfectly, and is brought to us to school to learn Latin, I would have him together with his Accidence, to be provided of this Book, in which he may at least once a day (beside his Accidence) be thus exercised.

1. Let him look over the pictures with their general titles and inscriptions, till he be able to turn readily to any one of them, and to tell its name either in English or Latin. By this means he shall have the method of the Book in his head; and be easily furnished with the knowledge of most things; and instructed how to call them, when at any time he meeteth with them elsewhere, in their real forms.

II. Let him read the description at large: First in English, and afterward in Latin, till he can readily read, and distinctly pronounce the words in both Languages, ever minding how they are spelled. And withal, let him take notice of the figures inserted, and to what part of the picture they direct by their like till he be well able to find out every particular thing of himself, and to name it on a sudden, either in English or Latin. Thus he shall not only gain the most primitive words, but be understandingly grounded in Orthography, which is a thing too generally neglected by us; partly because our English schools think that children should learn it at the Latin, and our Latin schools suppose they have already learn'd it at the English; partly, because our common Grammar is too much defective in this part, and scholars so little exercised therein, that they pass from schools to the Universities and return from thence (some of them) more unable to write true English, than either Latin or Greek. Not to speak of our ordinary Tradesmen, many of whom write such false English, that none but themselves can interpret what they scribble in their bills and shop-books.

III. Then let him get the Titles and Descriptions by heart, which he will more easily do, by reason of these impressions which the viewing of the pictures hath already made in his memory. And now let him also learn, 1. To construe, or give the words one by one, as they answer one another in Latin and English. 2. To Parse, according to the rules, (which I presume by this time) he hath learn'd in the first part of his Accidence; where I would have him tell what part of Speech any word is, and then what accidents belong to it; but especially to decline the nouns and conjugate the verbs according to the Examples in his Rudiments; and this doing will enable him to know the end and use of his Accidence. As for the Rules of Genders of Nouns, and the Praeter-perfect-tenses and Supines of Verbs, and those of Concordance and Construction in the latter part of the Accidence, I would not have a child much troubled with them, till by the help of this Book he can perfectly practise so much of Etymology, as concerns the first part of his Accidence only. For that, and this book together, being thoroughly learn'd by at least thrice going them over, will much prepare children to go cheerfully forward in their Grammar and School-Authors, especially, if whilst they are employed herein, they be taught also to write a fair and legible hand.

There is one thing to be given notice of, which I wish could have been remedied in this Translation; that the Book being writ in high-Dutch doth express many things in reference to that Country and Speech, which cannot without alteration of some Pictures as well as words be expressed in ours: for the Symbolical Alphabet is fitted for German children rather than for ours. And whereas the words of that Language go orderly one for one with the Latin, our English propriety of Speech will not admit the like. Therefore it will behove those Masters that intend to make use of this Book, to construe it verbatim to their young Scholars, who will quickly learn to do it of themselves, after they be once acquainted with the first words of Nouns, and Verbs, and their manner of variation.

Such a work as this, I observe to have been formerly much desired by some experienced Teachers, and I myself had some years since (whilst my own Child lived) begun the like, having found it most agreeable to the best witted Children, who are most taken up with Pictures from their Infancy, because by them the knowledge of things which they seem to represent (and whereof Children are as yet ignorant) are most easily conveyed to the Understanding. But for as much as the work is now done, though in some things not so completely as it were to be wished, I rejoyce in the use of it, and desist in my own undertakings for the present. And because any good thing is the better, being the more communicated; I have herein imitated a Child who is forward to impart to others what himself has well liked. You then that have the care of little Children, do not much trouble their thoughts and clog their memories with bare Grammar Rudiments, which to them are harsh in getting, and fluid in retaining; because indeed to them they signify nothing, but a mere swimming notion of a general term, which they know not what it meaneth, till they comprehend particulars, but by this or the like subsidiary, inform them, first with some knowledge of things and words wherewith to express them, and then their Rules of speaking will be better understood and more firmly kept in mind. Else how should a Child conceive what a Rule meaneth, when he neither knoweth what the Latin word importeth, nor what manner of thing it is which is signified to him in his own native Language, which is given him thereby to understand the Rule? For Rules consisting of generalities, are delivered (as I may say) at a third hand, presuming first the things, and then the words to be already apprehended touching which they are made. I might indeed enlarge upon this Subject, it being the very Basis of our Profession, to search into the way of Children's taking hold by little and little of what we teach them, that so we may apply ourselves to their reach: But I leave the observation thereof to your own daily exercise, and experience got thereby.

And I pray God, the fountain and giver of all wisdom, that hath bestowed upon us this gift of Teaching, so to inspire and direct us by his Grace, that we may train up Children in his Fear and in the knowledge of his Son Jesus Christ our Lord; and then no doubt our teaching and their learning of other things subordinate to these, will by the assistance of his blessed Spirit make them able and willing to do him faithful Service both in Church and Commonwealth, as long as they live here, that so they may be eternally blessed with him hereafter. This, I beseech you, beg for me and mine, as I shall daily do for you and yours, at the throne of God's heavenly grace; and remain while I live

Ready to serve you, as I truly love and honour you, and labour willingly in the same Profession with you, CHARLES HOOLE.

From my School, in

Lothbury, London, Jan. 25, 1658,

N. B. Those Heads or Descriptions which concern things beyond the present apprehension of Children's wits, as, those of Geography, Astronomy, or the like, I would have omitted, till the rest be learned, and a Child be *better able to understand them.*

The Judgment of Mr. Hezekiah Woodward, *sometimes an* eminent Schoolmaster in LONDON, *touching a work of this Nature; in his* Gate to Science, *chap.* 2.

Certainly *the use of Images or Representations is great:*

If we could make our words as legible to Children as Pictures are, their information therefrom would be quickned and surer. But so we cannot do, though we must do what we can. And if we had Books, wherein are the Pictures of all Creatures, Herbs, Beasts, Fish, Fowls, they would stand us in great stead. For Pictures are the most intelligible Books that Children can look upon. They come closest to Nature, nay, saith Scaliger, Art exceeds her.

An Advertisement Concerning this Edition

As there are some considerable Alterations in the present Edition of this Book from the former, it may be expected an Account should be given of the Reasons for them. 'Tis certain from the Author's Words, that when it was first published, which was in Latin and Hungary, or in Latin and High-Dutch; every where one word answer'd to another over-against it: This might have been observ'd in our English Translation, which wou'd have fully answer'd the design of COMENIUS, and have made the Book much more useful: But Mr. Hoole, (whether out of too much scrupulousness to disturb the Words in some places from the order they were in, or not sufficiently considering the Inconveniences of having the Latin and English so far asunder) has made them so much disagree, that a Boy has sometimes to seek 7 or 8 lines off for the corresponding Word; which is no small trouble to Young Learners who are at first equally unacquainted with all Words, in a Language they are strangers to, except it be such as have Figures of Reference, or are very like in sound; and thus may perhaps, innocently enough join an Adverb in one Tongue, to a Noun in the other; whence may appear the Necessity of the Translation's being exactly literal, and the two Languages fairly answering one another, Line for Line.

If it be objected, such a thing cou'd not be done (considering the difference of the Idioms) without transplacing Words here and there, and putting them into an order which may not perhaps be exactly classical; it ought to be observed, this is design 'd for Boys chiefly, or those who are just entering upon the Latin Tongue, to whom every thing ought to be made as plain and familiar as possible, who are not, at their first beginning, to be taught the elegant placing of Latin, nor from such short Sentences as these, but from Discourses where the Periods have a fuller Close. Besides, this way has already taken (according to the Advice of very good Judges,) in some other School-Books of Mr. Hoole's translating, and found to succeed abundantly well.

Such condescensions as these, to the capacities of young Learners are certainly very reasonable, and wou'd be most agreeable to the Intentions of the Ingenious and worthy Author, and his design to suit whatever he taught, to their manner of apprehending it. Whose Excellency in the art of Education made him so famous all over Europe, as to be solicited by several States and Princes to go and reform the Method of their Schools; and whose works carried that Esteem, that in his own Life-time some part of them were not only translated into 12 of the usual Languages of Europe, but also into the *Arabic, Turkish, Persian,* and *Mogolic* (the common Tongue of all that part of the East-Indies) and since his death, into the *Hebrew,* and some others. Nor did they want their due Encouragement here in *England,* some Years ago; 'till by an indiscreet use of them, and want of a thorow acquaintance with his Method, or unwillingness to part from their old road, they began to be almost quite left off: Yet it were heartily to be wish'd, some Persons of Judgment and Interest, whose Example might have an influence upon others, and bring them into Reputation again, wou'd revive the COMENIAN METHOD, which is no other, than to make our Scholars learn with Delight and cheerfulness, and to convey a solid and useful Knowledge of Things, with that of Languages, in an easy, natural and familiar way. *Didactic Works* (as they are now collected into one volume) for a speedy attaining the Knowledge of Things and Words, join'd with the Discourses of Mr. Lock [1] and 2 or 3 more out of our own Nation, for forming the Mind and settling good Habits, may doubtless be look'd upon to contain the most reasonable, orderly, and completed System of the Art of Education, that can be met with.

Yet, alas! how few are there, who follow the way they have pointed out? tho' every one who seriously considers it, must be convinc'd of the Advantage; and the generality of Schools go on in the same old dull road, wherein a great part of Children's time is lost in a tiresome heaping up a Pack of dry and unprofitable, or pernicious Notions (for surely little better can be said of a great part of that Heathenish stuff they are tormented with; like the feeding them with hard Nuts, which when they have almost broke their teeth with cracking, they find either deaf or to contain but very rotten and unwholesome Kernels) whilst Things really perfected of the understanding, and useful in every state of Life, are left unregarded, to the Reproach of our Nation, where all other Arts are improved and flourish well, only this of Education of Youth is at a stand; as if that, the good or ill management of which is of the utmost consequence to all, were a thing not worth any Endeavors to improve it, or was already so perfect and well executed that it needed none, when many of the greatest Wisdom and Judgment in several Nations, have with a just indignation endeavor'd to expose it, and to establish a more easy and useful way in its room.

'Tis not easy to say little on so important a subject, but thus much may suffice for the present purpose. The Book has merit enough to recommend itself to those who know how to make a right use of it. It was reckon'd one of the Author's best performances; and besides the many Impressions and Translations it has had in parts beyond Sea, has been several times re- printed here. It was endeavor'd no needless Alterations shou'd be admitted in this Edition, and as little of any as cou'd consist with the design of making it plain and useful; to shun the offence it might give to some; and only the Roman and Italic Character alternately made use of, where transplacing of Words cou'd be avoided.

London, J. H.
July 13, 1727.

[1] Mr. Lock's Essay upon Education, Dr. Tabor's Christian Schoolmaster, Dr. Ob. Walker of Education, Mr. Monro's Essay on Education. — His just Measures of the pious Institutions of Youth, &c.

Orbis Sensualium Pictus

A World of Things Obvious to the Senses drawn in Pictures

Invitation. - I. - Invitatio.

The Master and the Boy

M. Come, Boy, learn to be wise.
P. What doth this mean, *to be wise?*
M. To understand rightly, to do rightly, and to speak out rightly all that are necessary.
P. Who will teach me this?
M. I, by God's help.
P. How?
M. I will guide thee thorow all.
I will shew thee all.
I will name thee all.
P. See, here I am; lead me in the name of God.
M. Before all things, thou oughtest to learn the plain *sounds,* of which man's *speech* consisteth; which *living creatures* know how *to make,* and thy *Tongue* knoweth how *to imitate,* and thy hand can *picture out.*
Afterwards we will go into the *World,* and we will view all things.
Here thou hast a lively and Vocal Alphabet.

Magister & Puer

M. Veni, Puer, disce sapere.
P. Quid hoc est, *Sapere?*
M. Intelligere recte, agere recte, et eloqui recte omnia necessaria.
P. Quis docebit me hoc?
M. Ego, cum DEO.
P. Quomodo?
M. Ducam te per omnia.

Ostendam tibi omnia.
Nominabo tibi omnia.
P. En, adsum; due me in nomine DEI.
M. Ante omnia, debes discere simplices *Sonos* ex quibus *Sermo* humanus constat; quos *Animalia* sciunt *formare,* & tua *Lingua* scit *imitari,* & tua *Manus* potest *pingere.*
Postea ibimus *Mundum,* & spectabimus omnia.
Hic habes vivum et vocale Alphabetum.

Cornix cornicatur, à à
The *Crow* crieth.

Agnus balat, b è è è
The *Lamb* blaiteth.

Cicàda stridet, cì cì
The *Grasshopper* chirpeth.

Upupa dicit, du du
The *Whooppoo* saith.

Infans ejulat, è è è
The *Infant* crieth.

Ventus flat, fi fi
The *Wind* bloweth.

Anser gingrit, ga ga
The *Goose* gagleth.

Os halat, hà'h hà'h
The *Mouth* breatheth out.

Mus mintrit, ì ì ì
The *Mouse* chirpeth.

Anas tetrinnit, kha, kha
The Duck quaketh.

Lupus ululat, lu ulu
The *Wolf* howleth.

Ursus murmurat, [mum-mum
The *Bear* grumbleth.

Felis clamat, nau nau
The *Cat* crieth.

Auriga clamat, ò ò ò
The *Carter* crieth.

Pullus pipit, pi pi
The *Chicken* peepeth.

Cúculus cuculat, kuk ku
The *cuckow* singeth.

Canis ringitur, err
The *dog* grinneth.

Serpens sibilat. si
The *Serpent* hisseth.

Graculus clamat, tac tac
The *yay* crieth.

Bubo ululat, ù ù
The *Owl* hooteth.

Lepus vagit, va
The *Hare* squeaketh.

Rana coaxat, coax
The *Frog* croaketh.

Asinus rudit, , y y
The *Asse* brayeth.

Tabanus dicit, ds ds
The *Breeze* or *Horse-flie* saith.

God - II. - Deus.

God is of himself from everlasting to everlasting.

A most perfect and a most blessed *Being.*

In his *Essence* Spiritual, and One.

In his *Personality,* Three.

In his *Will,* Holy, Just, Merciful and True.

In his *Power* very great.

In his *Goodness,* very good.

In his *Wisdom,* unmeasurable.

A *Light* inaccessible; and yet all in all. Every where, and no where.

The chiefest *Good,* and the only and inexhausted Fountain of all good things.

As the *Creator,* so the *Governour* and *Preserver* of all things, which we call the *World.*

Deus est ex seipso, ab aeterno in seternum.

Perfectissimum & beatissimum *Ens.*

Essentiâ Spiritualis & unus.

Hypostasi Trinus.

Voluntate, Sanctus, Justus, Clemens, Verax.

Potentiâ maximus.

Bonitate Optimus.

Sapientiâ, immensus.

Lux inaccessa; & tamen omnia in omnibus. Ubique & nullibi.

Summum *Bonum,* et solus et inexhaustus Fons omnium Bonorum.

Ut *Creator,* ita *Gubernator* et *Conservator* omnium rerum,quas vocamus *Mundum.*

The World. - III. – Mundus.

The *Heaven,* 1. hath *Fire,* and *Stars.* The *Clouds,* 2. hang in the *Air.*
Birds, 3. fly under the Clouds. *Fishes,* 4. swim in the *Water.*
The *Earth* hath *Hills,* 5. *Woods,* 6. *Fields,* 7. *Beasts,* 8. and *Men,* 9.
Thus the greatest *Bodies* of the World, the four *Elements,* are full of their own Inhabitants.

Coelum, 1. habet *Ignem* & *Stellas. Nubes,* 2. pendent in *Aere. Aves,* 3. volant sub nubibus. *Pisces,* 4. natant in *Aqua. Terra* habet *Montes,* 5. *Sylvas,* 6. *Campos,* 7. *Animalia,* 8. *Homines,* 9. Ita maxima *Corpora* Mundi, quatuor *Elementa,* sunt plena Habitatoribus suis.

The Heaven. - IV. - Coelum.

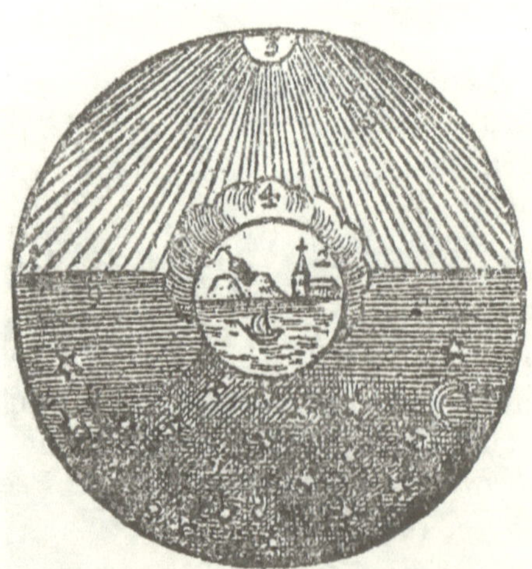

The *Heaven,* 1. is wheeled about, and encompasseth the *Earth.* 2. standing in the middle.

The Sun, 3. wheresoever it is, shineth perpetually, howsoever dark Clouds, 4. may take it from us; and causeth by his Rays, 5. Light, and the Light, Day,

On the other side, over against it, is Darkness, 6. and thence Night,

In the Night shineth the *Moon,* 7. and the *Stars,* 8. glister and twinkle.

In the Evening, 9. is *Twilight:*

In the *Morning,* 10. the breaking, and dawning of the Day.

Coelum, 1. rotatur, & ambit *Terram,* 2. stantem in medio.

Sol, 3. ubi ubi est, fulget perpetuo, ut ut *densa Nubila,* 4. eripiant eum a nobis; facitque suis *Radiis,* 5. *Lucem,* Lux *Diem.*

Ex opposito, sunt *Tenebrae,* 6. inde *Nox.*

Nocte splendet *Luna,* 7. & *Stellae,* 8. micant, scintillant.

Vesperi, 9. est *Crepusculum:*

Manè Aurora, 10. & Diluculum.

Fire. - V. - Ignis.

The *Fire* gloweth, burneth and consumeth to ashes.

A *spark* of it struck out of a *Flint* (or Firestone), 2. by means of a *Steel,* 1. and taken by *Tynder* in a *Tynder-box,* 3. lighteth a *Match,* 4. and after that a *Candle,* 5. or *stick,* 6. and causeth a *flame,* 7. or *blaze,* 8. which catcheth hold of the Houses.

Smoak, 9. ascendeth therefrom, which, sticking to the *Chimney,* 10. turneth into *Soot.*

Of a *Fire-brand,* (or burning stick) is made a *Brand,* 11. (or quenched stick).

Of a *hot Coal* (red hot piece of a Fire-brand) is made a *Coal,* 12. (or a *dead Cinder*) .

That which remaineth, is at last *Ashes* , 13. and *Embers* (or hot *Ashes*).

Ignis ardet, urit, cremat.

Scintilla ejus elisa e *Silice,* (Pyrite) 2. Ope *Chalybis,* 1. et excepta a *Fomite* in *Suscitabulo,* 3. accendit *Sulphuratum,* 4. et inde *Candelam,* 5. vel *Lignum,* 6. et excitat *Flammam,* 7. vel *Incendium,* 8. quod corripit AE dificia.

Fumus, 9. ascendit inde, qui, adhaerans Camino, 10. abit in Fuliginem.

Ex *Torre,* (ligno ardente,) fit *Titio,* 11. (lignum extinctum.)

Ex *Pruna,* (candente particulâ Torris,) fit *Carbo,* 12. (*Particula mortua.*)

Quod remanet, tandem est *Cinis,* 13. & *Favilla* (ardens *Cinis.*)

The Air – VI - Aër.

A cool *Air,* 1. breatheth gently.

The *Wind,* 2. bloweth strongly.

A *Storm,* 3. throweth down Trees.

A *Whirl-wind,* 4. turneth itself in a round compass.

A Wind *under Ground,* 5. causeth an *Earthquake.*

An Earthquake causeth gapings of the Earth, (and falls of Houses.) 6.

Aura, 1. spirat leniter.

Ventus, 2. flat valide.

Procella, 3. sternit xlrbores.

Turbo, 4. agit se in gyrum.

Ventus *subterraneus,* 5. excitat *Terrae motum.*

Terrae motus facit Labes (& ruinas.) 6.

The Water. - VII. - Aqua.

The Water springeth out of a *Fountain,* 1. floweth downwards in a *Brook,* 2. runneth in a *Beck,* 3. standeth in a *Pond,* 4. glideth in a *Stream,* 5. is whirled about in a *Whirl-pit,* 6. and causeth *Fens,* 7. The *River* hath *Banks,* 8.

The *Sea* maketh *Shores,* 9. *Bays,* 10, *Capes,* 11. *Islands,* 12. *Almost Islands,* 13. *Necks of Land,* 14. *Straights,* 15. and hath in it *Rocks,* 16.

Aqua scatet è *Fonte,* 1. defluit in *Torrente,* 2. manat in *Rivo,* 3. Stat in *Stagno,* 4. fluit in *Flumine,* 5. gyratur in *Vortice,* 6. & facit *Paludes,* 7. Flumen habet *Fipas.*

Mare facit *Littora,* 9. *Sinus,* 10. *Promontoria,* 11. *Insulas,* 12. *Peninsulas,* 13. *Isthmos,* 14. *Freta,* 15. & habet *Scopulos,* 16.

The Clouds. - VIII. - Nubes.

A *Vapour,* 1. ascendeth from the *Water.*

From it a *Cloud,* 2. is made, and a *white Mist,* 3. near the Earth.

Rain, 4. and a small *Shower* distilleth out of a *Cloud,* drop by drop.

Which being frozen, is *Hail,* 5. half frozen is *Snow,* 6. being warm is *Mel-dew.*

In a rainy Cloud, set over against the Sun the *Rainbow,* 7. appeareth.

A *drop* falling into the water maketh a *Bubble,* 8. many *Bubbles* make froth, 9.

Frozen Water is called *Ice,* 10. *Dew* congealed, is called a *white Frost.*

Thunder is made of a brimstone-like *vapour,* which breaking out of a Cloud, with *Lightning,* 11. thundereth and striketh with lightning.

Vapor, 1. ascendit ex *Aquâ.*

Inde *Nubes,* 2. fit, et *Nebula,* 3. prope terram.

Pluvia, 4. et *Imber,* stillat e *Nube,* guttatim.

Quae gelata, *Grando,* 5. semigelata, *Nix,* 6. calefacta, *Rubigo* est.

In nube pluviosâ, oppositâ soli *Iris,* 7. apparet.

Gutta aincidens in aquam, facit *Bullam,* 8. multae *Bullae* faciunt spumam, 9.

Aqua congelata *Glacies,* 10.

Ros congelatus, dicitur Fruina. Tonitru fit ex Vapor e sulphureo, quod erumpens e Nube cum Fulgure, ii, tonat & fulminat.

The Earth. - IX. - Terra.

In the *Earth* are high *Mountains,* 1. Deep *Vallies,* 2. *Hills* rising, 3. Hollow Caves, 4. Plain *Fields,* 5. Shady *Woods,* 6.

In *Terra* sunt Alti *Montes,* 1. Profundae *valles,* 2. Elevati Colles, 3. cavae Speluncae, 4. Plani *campi,* 5. Opacae Sylvae, 6.

The Fruits of the Earth. - X. - Terrae Foetus.

A *meadow,* 1. yieldeth grass with *Flowers* and *Herbs,* which being cut down, are made *Hay,* 2.

A *Field,* 3. yieldeth *Corn,* and Pot *herbs,* 4. *Mushrooms,* 5. *Straw-berries,* 6. *Myrtle-trees,* &c. *come up* in Woods.

Metals, Stones, and *Minerals* grow *under the earth.*

Pratum, 1. fert *Gramina,* cum *Floribus* & *Herbis* quae defecta fiunt *Foenum,* 2. *Arvum,* 3. fert *Fruges,* & *Olera,* 4. *Fungi,* 5. *Fraga,* 6. *Myrtilli,* &c. *Proveniunt* in Sylvis.

Metalla, Lapides, Mineralia, nascuntur sub terra.

Metals. - XI. - Metalla.

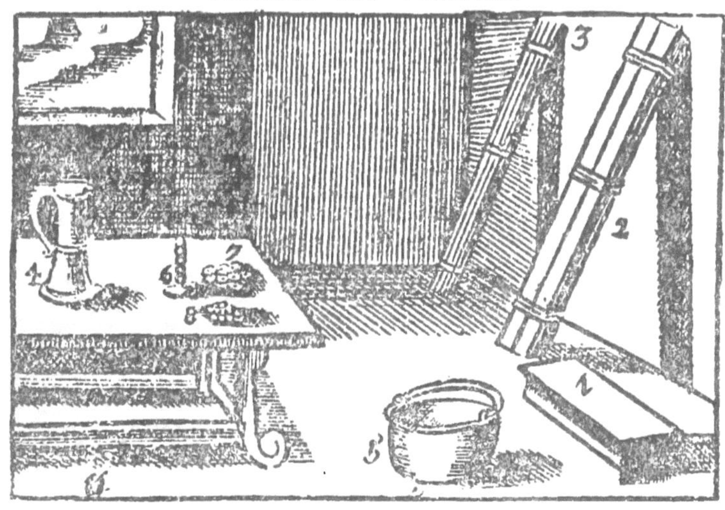

Lead, 1, is soft, and heavy.

Iron, 2. is hard, and *Steel,* 3. harder.

They make *Tankards* (or *Cans*), 4. of *Tin. Kettles,* 5. of *Copper, Candlesticks,* 6. of *Latin, Dollers,* 7. of *Silver, Ducats* and *Crown-pieces,* 8. *Quick-silver* is always liquid, and eateth thorow *Metals* of Gold.

Plumbum, 1. est molle & grave.

Ferrum, 2. est durum, & *Calybs,* 3. durior.

Faciunt *Cantharos,* 4, e *Stanno. Ahena,* 5, e *Cupro, Candelabra* ,6. ex *Orichalco, Thaleros,* 7. ex *Argento, Scutatos* et *Coronatos,* 8. Ex, *Auro. Argentum Vivum,* semper liquet, & corrodit *Metalla.*

Stones. – XII. - Lapides.

Sand, 1. and *Gravel,* 2. is Stone broken into bits.

A *great Stone,* 3. is a piece of a *Rock* (or Crag) 4.

A *Whetstone,* 5. a *Flint,* 6. a *Marble,* 7. &c. are ordinary Stones.

A *Load-stone,* 8. draweth Iron to it.

Jewels, 9. are clear Stones, as The *Diamond* white, The *Ruby* red, The *Sapphire* blue, The *Emerald* green, The *Jacinth* yellow, &c. And they glister being cut into corners.

Pearls and *Unions,* 10. grow in Shell-fish. *Corals,* 11. in a Sea-shrub. *Amber,* 12. is gathered from the Sea. *Glass,* 13. is like *Chrystal.*

Arena, 1. & *Sabulum,* 2. est *Lapis* comminutus. *Saxum,* 3. est pars *Petrae* (Cautis) 4. *Cos,* 5. *Silex,* 6. *Marmor,* 7. &c. sunt obscuri Lapides.

Magnes, 8. adtrahit ferrum. *Gemmae,* 9. sunt pellucidi Lapilli, ut *Adamas* candidus, *Rubinus* rubeus, *Sapphirus* caeruleus, *Smaragdus* viridis, *Hyacynthus* luteus, &c. et micant angulati.

Margaritae & *Uniones,* 10.. crescunt in Conchis. *Corallia,* 11. in Marinâ arbusculâ. *Succinum,* 12. colligitur è mari. *Vitrum,* 13. simile est *Chrystallo.*

Tree. - XIII. - Arbor.

A *Plant,* 1 . groweth from a *Seed.* A plant waxeth to a *Shoot*, 2.

A *Shoot* to a *Tree,* 3 .

The *Root,* 4. beareth up the Tree.

The *Body* or *Stem,* 5. riseth from the Root.

The *Stem* divideth it self into *Boughs,* 6. and green *Branches,* 7. made of *Leaves,* 8.

The *top,* 9. is in the height. The *Stock,* 10. is close to the roots.

A *Log,* 11. is the body fell'd down without Boughs; having *Bark* and *Rind,* 12. *Pith* and *Heart,* 13.

Bird-lime, 14. groweth upon the boughs, which also sweat *Gumm, Rosin, Pitch,* &c.

Planta, 1. procrescit e *Semine.* Planta abit in *Fruticem,* 2. *Frutex* in *Arborem,* 3. *Radix,* 4. Sustentat arborem.

Stirps (*Stemma*) 5. Surgit e radice. *Stirps* se dividit in *Ramos,* 6. & *Frondes,* 7. factas e *Foliis,* 8.

Cacumen, 9. est in summo. *Truncus,* 10. adhaerat radicibus.

Caudex, 11. est Stipes dejectus, sine ramis; habens *Corticem & Librum,* 12. *pulpam & medullam,* 13.

Viscum, 14. adnascitur *ramis,* qui etiam sudant, *Gummi, Resinam, Picem,* &c.

Fruits of Trees. - XIV. - Fructus Arborum.

Fruits that have no shells are pull'd from fruit-bearing trees.

The *Apple,* 1. is round.

The *Pear,* 2. and *Fig,* 3. are something long.

The *Cherry,* 4. hangeth by a long start.

The *Plumb,* 5. and *Peach,* 6. by a shorter.

The *Mulberry,* 7. by a very short one.

The *Wall-nut,* 8. the *Hazel-nut,* 9. and *Chest-nut,* 10. are wrapped in a *husk* and a *Shell,*

Barren trees are 11. The *Firr,* the *Alder,* The *Birch,* the *Cypress,* The *Beech,* the *Ash,* The *Sallow,* the *Linden-tree,* &c., but most of them affording shade.

But the *Juniper,* 12. and *Bay-tree,* 13. yield *Berries.*

The *Pine,* 14. *Pine-apples.*

The *Oak,* 15. *Acorns* and *Galls.*

Poma decerpuntur, a fructiferis arboribus.

Malum, 1. est rotundum.

Pyrum, 2. & *Ficus,* 3. sunt oblonga.

Cerasum, 4. pendet longo *Pediolo,*

Prunum, 5. & *Persicum,* 6. breviori.

Morum, 7. brevissimo.

Nux Juglans, 8. *Avellana,* 9. & *Castanea,* 10. involuta sunt *Cortici* & *Putamini.*

Steriles arbores sunt 11. *Abies, Alnus, Betula, Cupressus, Fagus, Fraxinus, Salix, Tilia,* &c. sed plerseque umbriferae.

At *Juniperus,* 12. & *Laurus,* 13. ferunt *Baccas.*

Pinus, 14. *Strobilos.*

Quercus, 15. *Glandes* & *Gallas.*

Flowers. – XV. - Flores.

Amongst the Flowers the most noted,

In the beginning of the Spring are the *Violet,* 1. the *Crow-toes,* 2. the *Daffodil,* 3.

Then the *Lillies,* 4. white and yellow and blew, 5. and the *Rose,* 6. and the *Clove-gilliflowers,* 7, &c.

Of these *Garlands,* 8. and *Nosegays,* 9. are tyed round with twigs.

There are added also *sweet herbs* , 10. as *Murjoram, Flower gentle, Rue, Lavender, Rosemary. Hysop, Spike, Basil, Sage, Mints,* &c.

Amongst Field-flowers, 11. the most noted are the *May-lillie, Germander,* the *Blew-Bottle, Chamomel,* &c.

And amongst Herbs, *Trefoil, Wormwood, Sorrel,* the *Nettle,* &c. The *Tulip,* 12. is the grace of flowers, but affording no smell.

Inter flores notissimi, Primo vere, *Viola,* 1. *Hyacinthus,* 2. *Narcissus,* 3.

Tum *Lilia,* 4. alba & lutea, & coerulea, 5. tandem *Rosa,* 6. & *Caryophillum,* 7. &c.

Ex his *Serta,* 8. & *Serviae,* 9. vientur. Adduntur etiam *Herbae odoratae,* 10. ut *Amaracus, Amaranthus, Ruta, Lavendula, Rosmarinus,* (Libanotis). *Hypossus, Nard, Ocymum, Salvia, Menta,* &c.

Inter Campestres Flores, 11. notissimi sunt *Lilium Convallium, Chamaedrys, Cyanus, Chamoemelum,* &c.

Et Herbae, *Cytisus* (Trifolium) *Absinthium, Acetosa, Urtica,* &c. *Tulipa,* 12. est decus Florum, sed expers odoris.

Potherbs. - XVI. - Olera.

Pot-herbs grow in Gardens, as *Lettice,* 1. *Colewort,* 2. *Onions,* 3. *Garlick,* 4. *Gourde,* 5. The *Parsnep,* 6. The *Turnep,* 7. The *Radish,* 8. *Horse-radish,* 9. *Parsly,* 10. *Cucumbers,* 11. and *Pompions,* 12.

Olera nascuntur in hortis, ut *Lactuca,* 1. *Brassica,* 2. *Cepa,* 3. *Allium,* 4. *Cucurbita,* 5. *Siser,* 6. *Rapa,* 7.

Raphanus minor, 8. *Raphanus major,* 9. *Petroselinum,* 10. *Cucumeres,* 11. *Pepones,* 12.

Corn. - XVII. - Fruges.

Some Corn grows upon a *straw,* parted by *knots,* as *Wheat,* 1. *Rie,* 2, *Barley,* 3. in which the *Ear* hath *awnes,* or else it is without awnes, and it nourisheth the *Corn* in the *Husk.*

Some instead of an ear, have a *rizom* (or plume) containing the corn by bunches, as *Oats,* 4. *Millet,* 5. *Turkey-wheat,* 6.

Pulse have *Cods,* which enclose the corns in two *Shales,* as *Pease,* 7. *Beans,* 8. *Vetches,* 9. and those that are less than these *Lentils* and *Urles* (or Tares).

Frumenta quaedam erescunt super *culmum,* distinctum *geniculis,* ut, *Triticum,* 1. *Siligo,* 2. *Hordeum,* 3. in quibus *Spica* habet *Aristas,* aut est mutica, fovetque *grana* in *gluma.*

Quaedam pro Spica, habent *Paniculam,* continentem grana fasciatim, ut, *Avena,* 4. *Milium,* 5. *Frumentum Saracenicum,* 6,

Legumina habent *Siliquas,* quae includunt grana *valvulis,* ut, *Pisum,* 7. *Fabae,* 8. *Vicia,* 9. & minores his *Lentes* & *Cicera.*

Shrubs. - XVIII. - Frutices.

A plant being greater, and harder than an herb, is called a *Shrub:* such as are in Banks and Ponds, the *Rush,* 1. the *Bulrush,* 2. or Cane without knots bearing *Cats-tails,* and the *Reed,* 3. which is knotty and hollow within.

Elsewhere, 4. the *Rose,* the *Bastard-Corinths,* the *Elder,* the *Juniper.*

Also the Vine, 5. which putteth forth *branches,* 6. and these *tendrels,* 7. *Vine-leaves,* 8. and Bunches of grapes, 9. on the stock whereof hang *Grapes,* which contain *Grape-stones.*

Planta major & durior herba, dicitur *Frutex:* ut sunt in ripis & stagnis, *Juncus,* 1. *Scirpus,* 2. [Canna] *enodis* ferens *Typhos,* & *Arundo,* 3. nodosa et cava intus.

Alibi, 4. *Rose, Ribes, Sambucus, Juniperus,*

Item *Vitis,* 5. quae emittit *Palmites,* 6. et hi *Capreolos,* 7. *Pampinos,* 8. et *Racemos,* 9. quorum Scapo pendent *Uvae,* continentes *Acinos.*

Living-Creatures: and First, Birds. - XIX. - Animalia: & primum. Aves.

A *living Creature* liveth, perceiveth, moveth itself; is born, dieth, is nourished, and groweth: standeth, or sitteth, or lieth, or goeth.

A *Bird,* (*Fisher,* 1. here the King's making her nest in the Sea.) is covered with *Feathers,* 2. flyeth with *Wings,* 3. hath two *Pinions,* 4. as many *Feet,* 5. a *Tail,* 6. and a *Bill,* 7. The *Shee,* 8. *layeth* Eggs, 10. in a nest, 9. and sitting upon them, hatcheth *young ones,* 11. An *Egg* is cover'd with a *Shell,* 12. under which is the *White,* 13. in this the *Yolk,* 14.

Animal vivit, sentit, movet se; nascitur, moritur, nutritur, & crescit; stat, aut sedet, aut cubat, aut graditur.

Avis, (hic Halcyon, 1. in mari nidulans.) tegitur *Plumis,* 2, volat *Pennis,* 3. habet duas *Alas,* 4. totidem *Pedes,* 5. *Caudam,* 6. & *Rostrum,* 7. *Foemella,* 8 . *ponit* Ova, 10. in nido, 9. et incubans iis, excludit *Pullos,* 11. *Ovum* tegitur *testa,* 12. sub qua est *Albumen,* 1 3 . in hoc *Vitellus,* 14.

Tame Fowls. - *XX.* - *Aves Domesticae*

The *Cock,* 1. (which croweth in the Morning.) hath a *Comb,* 2. and *Spurs,* 3. being gelded, he is called a *Capon,* and is crammed in a *Coop,* 4.

A *Hen,* 5, scrapeth the *Dunghil,* and picketh up Corns: as also the *Pigeons,* 6. (which are brought up in a *Pigeon-house,* 7.) and the *Turkey-cock,* 8. with his *Turkey-hen,* 9.

The gay *Peacock,* 10. prideth in his Feathers.

The *Stork,* 11. buildeth her nest on the top of the House,

The *Swallow,* 12. the *Sparrow,* 13. the *Mag-pie,* 14. the *Jackdaw,* 15. and the *Bat,* 16. (or Flettermouse) use to flie about Houses.

Gallus, 1. (qui cantat mane.) habet *Cristam,* 2. & *Calcaria,* 3. castratus dicitur *Capo* & saginatur in *Ornithotrophico,* 4.

Gallina, 5. ruspatur *fimetum,* & colligit grana: sicut & *Columbae,* 6, (quae educantur in *Columbario,* 7.) & *Gallopavus,* 8. cum sua *Meleagride,* 9.

Formosus *Pavo,* 10. superbit pennis.

Ciconia, 11. nidificat in tecto. *Hirundo,* 12. *Passer,* 13. *Pica,* 14. *Monedula,* 15. & *Vespertilio,* 16. (Mus alatus) volitant circa Domus.

Singing-Birds. – XXI. - Oscines.

The *Nightingal,* 1. singeth the sweetlyest of all.

The *Lark,* 2. singeth as she flyeth in the Air.

The *Quail,* 3. sitting on the ground; others on the boughs of trees, 4. as the *Canary-bird,* the *Chaffinch,* the *Goldfinch,* the *Siskin,* the *Linnet,* the little *Tit-mouse,* the *Wood-wall,* the *Robin-red-breast,* the *Hedge-sparrow,* &c.

The party colour'd *Parret,* 5. the *Black-bird,* 6. the *Stare,* 7. with the *Mag-pie* and the *Jay,* learn to frame men's words.

A great many are wont to be shut in *Cages,* 8.

Luscinia (*Philomela*), 1. cantatsuavissime omnium.

Alauda, 2. cantillat volitans in aere; *Coturnix,* 3. sedens humi;

Caeterse, in ramis arborum, 4. ut *Luteola* peregrina. *Fringilla, Carduelis, Acanthis, Linaria,* parvus *Parus, Galgulus, Rubecula, Curruca,* &c.

Discolor *Psittacus,* 5. *Merula,* 6. *Sturnus,* 7. cum *Pica,* & *Monedula,* discunt humanas voces formare Pleraeque solent includi *Caveis,* 8.

Birds that haunt the Fields and Woods. - XXII. - Aves Campestres & Sylvestres.

The *Ostrich,* 1. is the greatest Bird. The *Wren,* 2. is the least.

The *Owl,* 3. is the most despicable.

The *Whoopoo,* 4. is the most nasty, for it eateth dung.

The *Bird of Paradise,* 5. is very rare.

The *Pheasant,* 6. the *Bustard,* 7. the deaf wild *Peacock,* 8. the *Moor-hen,* 9. the *Partrige,* 10. the *Woodcock,* 11 . and the *Thrush,* 12. are counted Dainties.

Among the rest, the best are, the watchful *Crane,* 13. the mournful *Turtle,* 14. the *Cuckow,* 15. the *Stock-dove,* the *Speight,* the *Jay,* the *Crow,* &c, 16.

Struthio, 1. ales est maximus. *Regulus,* 2. (Trochilus) minimus.

Noctua, 3. despicatissimus.

Upupa, 4. sordidssimus, vescitur enim stercoribus.

Manucodiata, 5. rarissimus.

Phasianus, 6. *Tarda* (Otis), 7. surdus, *Tetrao,* 8. *Attagen,* 9. *Perdix,* 10. *Gallinago* (Rusticola), 11 & *Turdus,* 12, habentur in deliciis.

Inter reliquas, potissimse sunt, *Grus,* 13. pervigil. *Turtur,* 14. gemens. *Cuculus,* 15. *Palumbes, Picus, Garrulus, Comix,* &c, 16.

Ravenous Birds. - XXIII. - Aves Rapaces.

The *Eagle,* 1 . the King of Birds looketh upon the Sun, The *Vulture,* 2. and the *Raven,* 3. feed upon Carrion. The *Kite,* 4. pursueth Chickens. The *Falcon,* 5. the Hobbie, 6. and the Hawk, 7. catch at little Birds. The *Gerfalcon,* 8. catcheth Pigeons and greater Birds.

Aquila, 1. Rex Avium, intuetur Solem. Vultur, 2. & Corvus, 3. pascuntur *morticinis,* [cadaveribus.] *Milvus,* 4. insectatur pullos gallinaceos. *Falco,* 5, *Nisus,* 6. & *Accipiter,* 7. captant aviculas. *Astur,* 8. captat columbas & aves majores.

Water-Fowl. - XXIV. - Aves Aquaticae.

The white *Swan,* 1. the *Goose,* 2. and the *Duck,* 3. swim up and down.

The *Cormorant,* 4, diveth. And to these the waterhen,and the *Pelican,* &c, 10. The *Osprey,* 5. -and the *Sea-mew,* 6. flying downwards use to catch Fish, but the *Heron,* 7. standing on the Banks. The *Bittern,* 8, putteth his Bill in the water, and belloweth like an Ox. The *Water -wagtail,* 9. waggeth the tail.

Oler, 1. candidus, *Anser,* 2. & *Anas,* 3. natant. *Mergus,* 4. se mergit. Adde his Fulicam, *Pelecanum,* &c, 10. *Halioeetus,* 5. & *Gavia,* 6. devolantes, captant pisces, sed *Ardea,* 7. stans in ripis. *Butio,* 8. inferit rostrum aquae, & mugit ut bos. *Motacilla,* 9. motat caudam.

Flying Vermin. - XXV. - Insecta volantia.

The *Bee,* 1. maketh honey which the *Drone,* 2. devoureth. The *Wasp,* 3. and the *Hornet,* 4. molest with a sting; and the *Gad-Bee* (or Breese), 5. especially *Cattel;* but the *Fly,* 6. and the *Gnat,* 7. us. The *Cricket,* 8. singeth. The *Butterfly,* 9. is a winged *Caterpillar.* The *Beetle,* 10. covereth her wings with *Cases.* The *Glow-worm,* 11. shineth by night.

Apis, 1. facit mel quod *Fucus,* 2. depascit *Vespa,* 3. & *Crabro,* 4. infestant oculeo; & *Oestrum* (Asilus), 5. Imprimis *pecus,* autem *Musca,* 6. & *Culex,* 7. nos. *Gryllus,* 8. *cantillat. Papillio,* 9. est alata *Eruca. Scarabaeus,* 10. tegit alas *vaginis. Cicindela* [Lampyris], 11. nitet noctu.

Four-Footed Beasts: and First those about the House. - XXVI. - Quadrupeda: & primum Domestica.

The *Dog,* 1. with the *Whelp,* 2. is keeper of the House. The *Cat,* 3. riddeth the House of *Mice,* 4. which also a *Mouse-trap,* 5. doth, A *Squirrel,* 6. The *Ape,* 7. and the *Monkey,* 8. are kept at home for delight.

The *Dormouse,* 9. and other greater Mice, 10. as, the *Weesel,* the *Marten,* and the *Ferret,* trouble the House.

Canis, 1. cum *Catello,* 2. est custos Domiis. *Felis* (Catus) 3. purgat domum à *Muribus,* 4. quod etiam *Muscipula,* 5. facit. *Sciurus,* 6. *Simia,* 7. & *Cercopithecus,* 8. habentur domi delectamento. *Glis,* 9. & caeteri Mures majores, 10. ut, *Mustela, Martes, Viverra,* infestant domum.

Herd-Cattle. - XXVI. - Pecora.

The *Bull,* 1. the *Cow,* 2. and the *Calf,* 3. are covered with hair.

The *Rain,* the *Weather,* 4. The *Ewe,* 5. and the *Lamb,* 6. bear wool.

The *He-goat,* the *Gelt-goat,* 7. with the *She-goat,* 8. and *Kid,* 9. have *shag-hair* and *beards.*

The *Hog,* the *Sow,* 10. and the *Pigs,* 11. have *bristles,* but not *horns;* but also *cloven feet* as those others (have.)

Taurus, 1. *Vacca,* 2. & *Vitulus,* 3. teguntur pilis.

Aries, Vervex, 4. *Ovis,* 5. cum *Agno,* 6. gestant lanam. *Hircus, Caper,* 7. cum *Capra,* 8. & *Hoedo,* 9. habent. *Villos* & *aruncos.*

Porcus, Scrofa, 10. cum *Porcellis,* 11. habent *Setas,* at non *Cornua;* sed etiam *Ungulas bisulcas* ut ilia.

Labouring Beasts. - XXVIII.

The *Ass,* 1. and the *Mule,* 2. carry burthens.

The *Horse,* 3. (which a *Mane,* 4. graceth) carryeth us.

The *Camel,* 5. carryeth the Merchant with his Ware.

The *Elephant,* 6. draweth his meat to him with his *Trunk,* 7.

He hath two *Teeth,* 8. standing out, and is able to carry full thirty men.

Asinus, 1. & *Mulus,* 2. gestant Onera.

Equus, 3. (quam *Juba,* 4. ornat) gestat nos ipsos.

Camelus, 5. gestat Mercatorem cum mercibus suis.

Elephas, (Barrus) 6. attrahit pabulum *Proboscide,* 7.

Habet duos *dentes,* 8. prominentes, & potest portare etiam triginta viros.

Wild-Cattle. - XXIX. - Ferae Pecudes.

The *Buff,* 1. and the *Buffal,* 2. are wild Bulls.

The *Elke,* 3. being bigger than an Horse (whose back is impenetrable) hath knaggy horns as also the *Hart,* 4. but the *Roe,* 5. and the *Hind-calf,* almost none. The *Stone-back,* 6. huge great ones.

The *Wild-goat,* 7. hath very little ones, by which she hangeth her self on a Rock.

The *Unicorn,* 8, hath but one, but that a precious one.

The *Boar,* 9. assaileth one with his tushes.

The *Hare,* 10. is fearful.

The *Cony,* 11. diggeth the Earth.

As also the *Mole,* 12. which maketh hillocks.

Urus, 1. & *Bubalus,* 2. sunt feri Boves.

Alces, 3. major equo (cujustergusest impenetrabilis) habet ramosacornua; ut & *Cervus,*4.

Sed *Caprea,* 5. cum *Hinnulo,* ferè nulla.

Capricornus, 6. praegrandia; *Rupicapra,* 7. minuta, quibus suspendit se ad rupem.

Monoceros, 8. habet unum, sed pretiosum. *Aper,* 9. grassatur dentibus. *Lepus,* 10. pavet. *Cuniculus,* 11. perfodit *terram;* Ut & *Talpa,* 12. quae facit grumos.

Wild-Beasts. - XXX. - Ferae Besitae.

Wild Beasts have sharp paws, and teeth, and are flesh eaters.

As the *Lyon,* 1. the King of four-footed Beasts, having a mane; with the *Lioness.* The spotted *Panther,* 2. The *Tyger,* 3. the cruellest of all. The Shaggy *Bear,* 4. The ravenous *Wolf,* 5. The quick sighted *Ounce,* 6. The tayled *fox,* 7. the craftiest. The *Hedge-hog,* 8. is prickly. The *Badger,* 9. delighteth in holes.

Bestiac habent acutos ungues, & dentes, suntque carnivorae,

Ut *Leo,* 1 . Rex quadrupedum, jubatus; cum *Leoenâ.* Maculosus, *Pardo* (Panthera) 2. *Tygris,* 3. immanissima omnium. Villosus *Ursus,* 4. Rapax *Lupus,* 5. *Lynx,* 6. visu pollens, Caudata *Vulpes,* 7. astutissima *omnium. Erinaceus,* 8. est aculeatus. *Melis,* 9. gaudet latebris.

Serpents and Creeping things. - XXXI. - Serpentes & Reptilia.

Snakes creep by winding themselves; The *Adder,* 1. in the wood; The *Water-snake,* 2. in the water; The *Viper,* 3. amongst great stones. The *Asp,* 4. in the fields. The *Boa,* (or Mild-snake) 5. in Houses. The *Slow-worm,* 6. is blind.

The *Lizzard,* 7. and the *Salamander,* 8. (that liveth long in fire) have feet. The *Dragon,* 9. a *winged Serpent,* killeth with his Breath. The *Basilisk,* 10. with his Eyes; And the *Scorpion,* 11. with his poysonous tail.

Angues repunt sinuando se; *Coluber,* 1. in Sylvâ; *Natrix,* (hydra) 2. in Aquâ; *Vipera,* 3. in saxis; *Aspis,* 4,in campis. *Boa,* 5. in Domibus. *Coecilia,* 6. est coeca. *Lacerta,* 7. *Salamandra,* 8, (in igne vivax,) habent pedes. *Draco,* 9. *Serpens alatus,* necat halitu. *Basiliscus,* 10. Oculis; *Scorpio,* 11. venenata cauda.

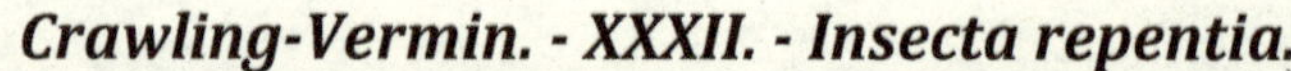

Crawling-Vermin. - XXXII. - Insecta repentia.

Worms gnaw *things.* The *Earth-worm,* 1. the Earth. The *Caterpillar,* 2. the Plant. The *Grashopper,* 3. the Fruits. The *Mite,* 4. the Corn. The *Timber-worm,* 5. Wood. The *Moth,* 6. a garment. The *Book-worm,* 7. a Book. *Maggots,* 8. Flesh and Cheese. *Hand-worms,* the Hair. The skipping *Flea,* 9. the *Lowse,* 10. and the stinking *Wall-louse,* 11. bite us. The *Tike,* 12. is a blood-sucker. The *Silk-worm,* 13. maketh silk. The *Pismire,* 14. is painful. The *Spider,* 15. weaveth a Cobweb, nets for flies. The *Snail,* 16. carrieth about her Snail-horn.

Vermes, rodunt *res.*

Lumbricus, 1. terram. *Eruca,* 2. plantam. *Cicada,* 3. Fruges. *Circulio,* 4. Frumenta. *Teredo,* (cossis) 5. Ligna. *Tinea,* 6. vestem. *Blatta,* 7. Librum. *Termites,* 8. carnem & caseum. *Acari,* Capillum. Saltans *Pulex,* 9. *Pediculus,* 10. foetans *Cimex,* 11. mordent nos. *Ricinus,* 12. sanguisugus est. *Bombyx,* 13. facit sericum. *Formica,* 14. est laboriosa. *Aranea,* 15. texit Araneum, retia muscis. *Cochlea,* 16. circumfert testam.

Creatures that live as well by Water as by Land. - XXXIII. - Amphibia.

Creatures that live by land and by water, are The *Crocodile,* 1. a cruel and preying Beast of the River Nilus; The *Castor* or *Beaver,* 2. having feet like a Goose, and a scaly tail to swim. The *Otter,* 3. The croaking *Frog,* 4. with the *Toad.* The *Tortoise,* 5. covered above and beneath with shells, as with a target.

Viventia in terrâ & aquâ, sunt *Crocodilus,* 1. immanis & praedatrix bestia *Nili* fluminis; *Castor,* (Fiber) 2. habens pedes anserinos & squameam Caudam ad natandum. *Lutra,* 3. & coaxans *Rana,* 4. cum *Bufone. Testudo,* 5. Operta & infra, testis, ceu scuto.

River Fish and Pond Fish. - XXXIV. - Pisces Fluviatiles & Lacustres.

A *Fish* hath *Fins,* 1. with which it swimmeth, and *Gills,* 2. by which it taketh breath, and *Prickles* instead of bones: besides the *Male* hath a *Milt,* and the *Female* a *Row.*

Some have *Scales,* as the *Carp,* 3. and the *Luce* or *Pike,* 4.

Some are sleek as the *Eel,* 5. and the *Lamprey,* 6.

The *Sturgeon,* 7. having a sharp snout, groweth beyond the length of a Man.

The *Sheath-fish,* 8. having wide Cheeks, is bigger than he:

But the greatest, is the *Huson,* 9. *Minews,* 10. swimming by shoals, are the least.

Others of this sort are the *Perch,* the *Bley,* the *Barbel,* the *Esch,* the *Trout,* the *Gudgeon,* and *Trench,* 11. The *Crab-fish,* 12. is covered with a shell, and it hath *Claws,* and crawleth forwards and backwards. The *Horse-leech,* 13. sucketh blood.

Piscis habet *Pinnas,* 1. quibus natat; & *Branchias,* 2. quibus respirat; & *Spinas* loco ossium: praeterea, *Mas Lactes, Foemina Ova.*

Quidam habent *Squamas,* ut *Carpio,* 3. *Lucius,* (Lupus) 4.

Alii sunt glabri, ut, *Anguilla,* 5. *Mustela,* 6.

Accipenser (Sturio), 7. mucronatus, crescit ultra longitudinem viri.

Silurus, 8. bucculentus, major illo est: Sed maximus *Antaseus* (Huso,) 9.

Apuae, 10. natantes gregatim, sunt minutissimae.

Alii hujus generis sunt *Perca, Alburnus, Mullus,* (Barbus) *Thymallus, Trutta, Gobius, Tinea,* 11. *Cancer,* 12. tegitur *crusta,* habetque *chelas,* & graditur porro & retrò. *Hirudo,* 13. sugit sanguinem.

Sea-fish, and Shell-fish. - XXXV. - Marini pisces & Conchae.

The *Whale,* 1. is the greatest of the Sea fish.

The *Dolphin,* 2. the swiftest. The *Scate,* 3. the most monstrous.

Others are the *Lamprel,* 4. the *Salmon,* or the *Lax,* 5.

There are also fish that flie, 6. Add *Herrings,* 7. which are brought pickled, and *Place,* 8. and *Cods,* 9. which are brought dry; and the Sea monsters, the *Seal.* 10. and the *Sea-horse,* &c. *Shell-fish,* 11. have Shells. The *Oyster,* 12. affordeth sweet meat. 13. *Purple-fish,* 13. purple; The others, Pearls, 14.

Baloena, (Cetus) 1. maximus Piscium marinorum. *Delphinus,* 2. velocissimus. *Raia,* 3. monstrossimus. Alii sunt *Muraenula,* 4. *Salmo,* (Esox) 5. Danturetiam volatiles, 6. Adde *Haleces,* 7. qui salsi, & *Passeres,* 8. cum *Asellis,* 9. qui adferuntur arefacti; & monstra marina, *Phocam,* 10. *Hippopotamum,* &c. *Concha,* 1 1 . habet testas, *Ostrea,* 12. dat sapidam carnem. *Murex,* 13. purpuram; *Alii,* 14. Margaritas.

Man. - XXXVI. - Homo.

Adam, 1. the first Man, was made by God after his own Image the sixth day of the Creation, of a lump of Earth.

And *Eve,* 2. the first Woman, was made of the Rib of the Man.

These, being tempted by the *Devil* under the shape of a *Serpent,* 3. when they had eaten of the fruit of the *forbidden Tree,* 4. were condemned, 5. to misery and death, with all their posterity, and cast out of *Paradise,* 6.

Adamus, 1. primus Homo, formatus est a Deo ad Imaginem suam sextâ die Creationis, e Gleba Terrae.

Et *Eva,* 2. prima mulier, formata est e costâ viri.

Hi, seducti *abolo* sub specie *Serpentis,* 3. cum comederent de fructu *vetitae arboris,* 4. damnati sunt, 5. ad miseriam & mortem, cum omni posteritate sua, & ejecti e *Paradiso* 6.

The Seven Ages of Man. - XXXVII. -Septem States Hominis.

A Man is first an *Infant,* 1. then a *Boy,* 2. then a *Youth,* 3. then a *Young-man,* 4. then a *Man,* 5. after that an *Elderly-man,* 6. and at last, a *decrepid old man,* 7.

So also in the other *Sex,* there are, a *Girl,* 8. A *Damosel,* 9. a *Maid,* 10. A *Woman,* 11. an elderly *Woman,* 12. and a *decrepid old Woman,* 13.

Homo est primum *Infans,* 1 . deinde *Puer,* 2. tum *Adolescens,* 3. inde *Juvenis,* 4. posteà *Vir,* 5. dehinc *Senex,* 6. tandem *Silicernium,* 7.

Sic etiam in altero *Sexu,* sunt, *Pupa,* 8. *Puella,* 9. *Virgo,* 10, *Mulier,* 11. *Vetula,* 12. *Anus decrepita,* 13.

The Outward Parts of a Man. - XXXVIII. - Membra Hominis Externa.

The *Head,* 1. is above, the *Feet,* 20. Below, the fore part of the Neck (which ends at the *Arm-Holes,* 2.) is the *Throat,* 3. the hinder part, the *Crag,* 4.

The *Breast,* 5, is before; the *back,* 6, behind; Women have in it two *Dugs,* 7. with *Nipples,*

Under the Breast is the *Belly,* 9. in the middle of it the *Navel,* 10. underneath the *Groyn,* 11. and the *privities.*

The *Shoulder-blades,* 12. are behind the back, on which the *Shoulders* depend, 13. on these the *Arms,* 14. with the *Elbow,* and then on either side the *Hands,* the right, 8. and the left, 16, The *Loyns* are next the Shoulders, with the *Hips,* 18. and in the *Breech,* the *Buttocks,* 19.

These make the *Foot;* the *Thigh,* 2 1. then the *Leg,* 23. (the *Knee,* being betwixt them, 22.) in which is the *Calf,* 24. with the *Shin,* 25. then the *Ankles,* 26. the *Heel,* 27. and the *Sole,* 28. in the very end, the great *Toe,* 29. with four (other) *Toes.*

Caput, 1. est supra, infra *Pedes,* 20. Anterior pars Colli (quod desit in *Axillas,* 2.) est *Jugulum,* 3. posterior *Cervix,* 4.

Pectus, 5. est ante; *Dorsum,* 6. retro; Foeminis sunt in illo binae *Mammae,* 7. cum *Papillis.*

Sub pectore est *Venter,* 9. in ejus medio, *Umbelicus,* 10. subtus *Inguen,* 11. & *pudenda. Scapulae,* 12, sunt a tergo, â quibus pendent *humeri,* 13. ab his *Brachia,* 14. cum *Cubito,* 15. inde ad utrumque Latus, *Manus, Dextera,* 8. & *Sinistra,* 16. *Lumbi,* 17. excipiunt Humeros, cum *Coxis,* 18. & in *Podice,* (culo) *Nates,* 19. Absolvunt Pedem; *Femur,* 21. tum *Crus,* 23. (*Genu,* 22. intermedio.) in quo *Sura,* 24. cum *Tilia,* 25. abhinc *Tali,* 26. *Calx,* (Calcaneum) 27. & *Solum,* 28. in extremo *Hallux,* 29. cum quatuor *Digitis.*

The Head and the Hand. - XXXIX. - Caput & Manus.

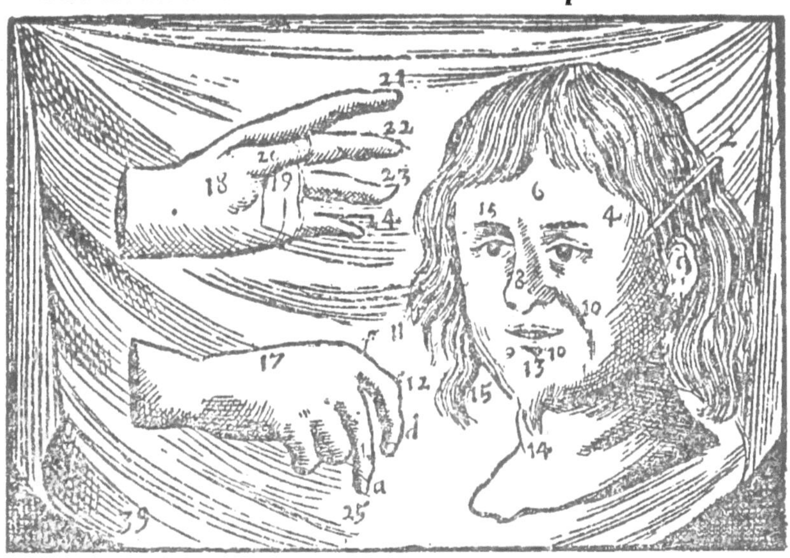

In the *Head* are the *Hair,* 1. (which is combed with a *Comb,* 2.) two *Ears,* 3. the *Temples,* 4. and the *Face,* 5.

In the Face are the *Fore-head,* 6. both the *Eyes,* 7. the *Nose,* 8. (with two *Nostrils)* the *Mouth,* 9. the *Cheeks,* 10. and the *Chin,* 13.

The *Mouth* is fenced with a *Mustacho,* 11. and *Lips,* 12.

A *Tongue* and a *Palate,* and *Teeth,* 16. in the *Cheek-bone.*

A Man's Chin is covered with *Beard,* 14. and the Eye (in which is the *White* and the *Apple*) with *eye-lids,* and an *eye-brow,* 15.

The *Hand* being closed is a *Fist,* 17. being open is a *Palm,* 18. in the midst, is the *hollow,* 19. of the Hand, the extremity is the *Thumb,* 20. with four Fingers, the *Fore-finger,* 21. the *Middle-finger,* 22. the *Ring-finger,* 23. and the *Little-finger,* 24.

In every one are three *joynts,* a. b. c. and as many *knuckles,* d.e.f. with a *Nail,* 25.

In *Capite* sunt *Capillus,* 1. (qui pectitur *Pectine,* 2.) *Aures,* 3. binae, & *Tempora,* 4. *Facies,* 5. In facie sunt *Frons,* 6. *Oculus,* 7. uterque, *Nasus,* 8. (cum duabus *Naribus*) *Os,* 9. *Genae,* (Malae) 10. & *Mentum,* 13. Os septum est *Mystace,* 11. & *Labiis,* 12.

Lingua cum *Palato, Dentibus,* 16. in *Maxilla,* Mentum virile tegitur *Barba,* 14. Oculos vero (in quo *Albugo* & *Pupilla*) *palpaebris,* & *supercilio,* 15. *Manus* contracta, *Pugnus,* 17. est aperta, *Palma,* 18. in medio *Vola,* 19. extremitas, *Pollex,* 20. cum quatuor *Digitis, Indice,* 21. *Medio,* 22. *Annulari,* 23. & *Auriculari,* 24.

In quolibet sunt *articuli* tres, a. b. c. & totidem *Condyli,* d. e. f. cum *Ungue,* 25.

The Flesh and Bowels. – XL. - Caro & Viscera.

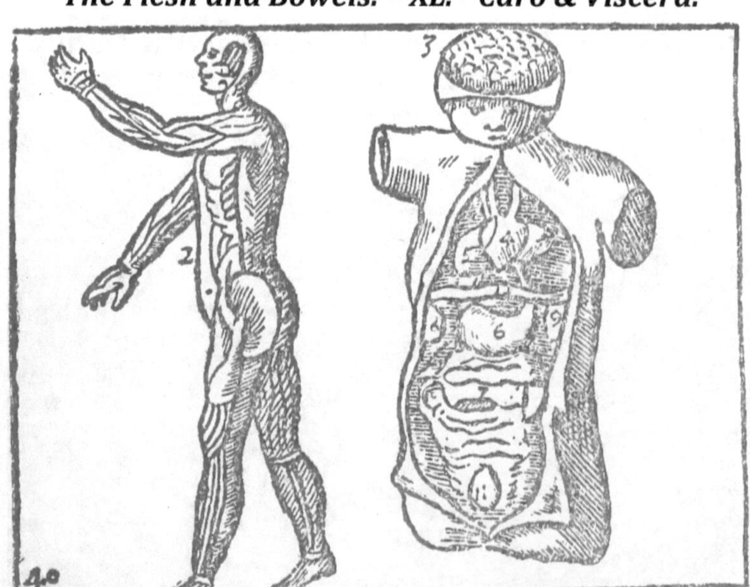

In the *Body* are the *Skin* with the *Membranes,* the *Flesh* with the *Muscles,* the *Chanels,* the *Gristles,* the *Bones* and the *Bowels.*

The *Skin,* 1. being pull'd off, the *Flesh,* 2. appeareth, not in a continual lump, but being distributed, as it were in stuft puddings, which they call *Muscles,* whereof thereare reckoned four hundred and five, being the Chanels of the *Spirits,* to move the *Members.*

The *Bowels* are the inward *Members:* As in the Head, the *Brains,* 3. being compassed about with a *Skull,* and the *Skin* which covereth the *Skull.* In the Breast, the *Heart,* 4. covered with a thin *Skin* about it, and the *Lungs,* 5. breathing to and fro. In the Belly, the *Stomach,* 6. and the *Guts,* 7. covered with a *Caul.* The *Liver,* 8. and in the left side opposite against it, the *Milt,* 9. the two *Kidneys,* 10. and the *Bladder,* 11.

The Breast is divided from the Belly by a thick Membrane, which is called the *Mid-riff,* 12.

In *Corpore* sunt *Cutis* cum *Membranis, Caro* cum *Musculis, Canales, Cartilagines, Ossa* & *Viscera.*

Cute, 1. detractâ, *Caro,* 2, apparet, non continuâ massâ, sed distributa, tanquam in farcimina, quos vocant *Musculos,* quorum numerantur *quadringenti quinque,* canales *Spirituum,* ad movendum *Membra.*

Viscera sunt *Membra* interna: Ut in Capite, *Cerebrum,* 3. circumdatum *Cranio,* & *Pericranio.* In Pectore, *Cor,* 4. obvolutum *Pericardio,* & *Pulmo,* 5. respirans. In *Ventre, Ventriculus,* 6. & *Intestina,* 7. obdacta *Omento. Jecur,* (Hepar) 8. & à sinistro oppositus ei *Lien,* 9. duo *Renes,* 10, cum *Vesica,* 11.

Pectus dividitur à Ventre crassâ Membranâ, quae vocatur *Diaphragma,* 12.

The Chanels and Bones. - XLI. - Canales & Ossa.

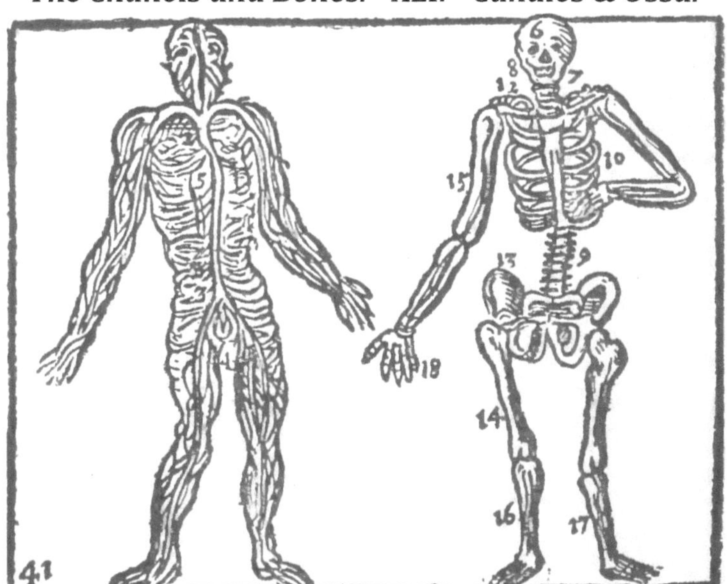

The Chanels of the Body are the *Veins,* carrying the Blood from the Liver;

The *Arteries* (carrying) *Heart* and *Life* from the *Heat;*

The *Nerves* (carrying) Sense and Motion throughout the Body from the *Brain.*

You shall find these three, 1. everywhere joined together.

Besides, from the Mouth into the Stomach is the *Gullet,* 2. the way of the meat and drink; and by it to the Lights, the *Wezand,* 5. for breathing; from the Stomach to the Anus is a great *Intestine,* 3. to purge out the *Ordure;* from the Liver to the Bladder, the *Ureter,* 4. for making water.

The *Bones* are in the Head, the *Skull,* 6. the two *Cheek-bones,* 7. with thirty-two *Teeth,* 8.

Then the *Back-bone,* 9. the Pillar of the Body, -consisting of thirty-four turning *Joints,* that the Body may bend it self.

The *Ribs,* 10. whereof there are twenty-four.

The *Breast-bone,* 11. the two *Shoulder-blades,* 12. the *Buttock-bone,* 13. the *bigger Bone* in the Arm, 15. and the *lesser Bone* in the Arm.

The *Thigh bone,* 14. the foremost, 16. and the hindmost Bone, in the Leg, 17. The Bones of the Hand, 18. are thirty-four, and of the Foot, 19. thirty.

The *Marrow* is in the Bones.

Canales Corporis sunt *Venae* deferentes Sanguinem ex Hepate; *Arteriae, Calorem* & *Vitam è Corde; Nervi,* Sen sum et Motum, per Corpus a *Cerebro.*

Invenies haec tria, 1. ubique sociata.

Porrò, ab Ore in Ventriculum *Gula,* 2. via cibi ac potus; & juxta hanc, ad Pulmonem *Guttur,* 5. pro respiratione; à ventriculo ad Anum *Colon,* 3. ad ex-cernendum *Stercus;* ab Hepate ad Vesicam, *Ureter,* 4. reddendae urinae.

Ossa sunt in Capite, *Calvaria,* 6. duae *Maxillae,* 7. cum XXXII. *Dentibus,* 8.

Tum, *Spina dorsi,* 9. columna Corporis, constans ex XXXIV. *Vertebris,* ut Corpus queat flectere se *Costae,* 10. quarum viginti quatuor,

Os Pectoris, 11. duae *Scapulae,* 12. *Os sessibuli,* 13. *Lacerti,* 15. & *Ulna.*

Tibia, 14. *Fibula,* 16. anterior, & posterior, 17. Ossa Manûs, 18. sunt triginta quatuor, Pedis, 19. triginta. *Medulla* est in Ossibus.

The Outward and Inward Senses. - XLII. - Sensus exter

There are five outward Senses;

The *Eye,* 1. seeth Colours, what is white or black, green or blew, red or yellow.

The *Ear,* 2. heareth *Sounds,* both natural. Voices and Words; and artificial, Musical Tunes.

The *Nose,* 3. scenteth smells and stinks.

The *Tongue,* 4. with the roof of the Mouth tastes *Savours,* what is sweet or bitter, keen or biting, sower or harsh.

The *Hand,* 5. by touching discerneth the quantity and quality of things; the hot and cold, the moist and dry, the hard and soft, the smooth and rough, the heavy and light.

The inward *Senses* are three.

The *Common Sense,* 7. under the *forepart of the head,* apprehendeth things taken from the outward Senses.

The *Phantasie,* 6. under the *crown of the head* judgeth of those things, thinketh and dreameth,

The *Memory,* 8. under the *hinder part of the head,* layeth up every thing and fetcheth them out: it loseth some, and this is *forgetfulness.*

Sleep, is the rest of the Senses.

Sunt quinque externi *Seiisus;*

Oculus, 1. videt *Colores,* quid album vel atrum, viride vel coeruleum, rubrum aut luteum, sit.

Auris, 2. audit *Sonos,* tum naturales. Voces & Verba; tum artificiales,

Tonos Musicos,

Nasus, 3, *olfacit* odores & foetores.

Lingua, 4. cum Palato gustat *Sapores,* quid dulce aut amarum, acre aut acidum, acerbum aut austerum.

Manus, 5. tangendo dignoscit quantitatem, & qualitatem rerum; calidum & frigidum, humidum & siccum, durum & molle, laeve & asperum, grave & leve.

Sensus interni sunt tres.

Sensus Communis, 7. sub *sincipite* apprehendit res perceptas a Sensibus externis.

Phantasia, 6. sub *vertice,* dijudicat res istas, cogitat, somniat.

Memoria, 8. sub *occipitio,* recondit singula & depromit: deperdit quaedam, & hoc est *oblivio.*

Somnus, est requies Sensuum.

The Soul of Man. - XLIII. - Anima hominis.

The *Soul* is the Life of the Body,one in the whole. Only *Vegetative* in *Plants;*

Withal *Sensitive* in *Animals;* And also rational in *Men.*

This consisteth in three things;

In the *Understanding,* whereby it judgeth and understandeth a thing good and evil, or true, or apparent.

In the *Will,* whereby it chooseth, and desireth, or rejecteth, and misliketh a thing known.

In the *Mind,* whereby it pursueth the Good chosen or avoideth the Evil rejected.

Hence is *Hope* and *Fear* in the desire, and dislike.

Hence is *Love* and *Joy,* in the Fruition:

But *Anger* and *Grief,* in suffering.

The true judgment of a thing is *Knowledge;* the false, is *Error, Opinion* and *Suspicion.*

Anima est vita corporis, una in toto.
Tantùm *Vegetativa* in *Plantis;* Simul *Sensitiva* in *Animalibus;*
Etiam *Rationalis* in *Homine.* Haec consistet in tribus:
In *Mente* (Intellectu) quâ cognoscit, & intelligit, bonum ac malum, vel verum, vel apparens.
In *Voluntate,* quâ eligit, & concupiscit, aut rejicit, & aversatur cognitum.
In *Animo,* quo prosequitur Bonum electum, vel fugit Malum rejectum.
Hinc *Spes* & *Timor,* in cupidine, & aversatione:
Hinc *Amor* & *Gaudium,* in fruitione: Sed *Ira* ac *Dolor,* in passione.
Vera cognitio rei, est *Scientia;* falsa, *Error, Opinio, Suspicio.*

Deformed and Monstrous People. - XLIV. - Deformes & Monstrosi.

Monstrous and *deformed* People are those which differ in the Body from the ordinary shape, as the huge *Gyant,* 1. the little *Dwarf,* 2. One with *two Bodies,* 3. One with *two Heads,* 4. and such like Monsters.
Amongst these are reckoned, The *jolt-headed,* 5. The great *nosed,* 6. The *blubber-lipped,* 7. The *blub-cheeked,* 8. The *goggle-eyed,* 9. The *wry-necked,* 10. The *great-throated,* 1 1 . The *Crump-backed,* 12. The *Crump-footed,* 13. The *steeple-crowned,* 15. add to these The *Bald-pated,* 14.

Monstrosi, & *deformes* sunt abeuntes corpore a communi formâ, ut sunt, immanis *Gigas,* nanus (*Pumilio*), 2. *Bicorpor,* 3. *Biceps,* 4. & id genus monstra.
His accensentur, *Capito,* 5. *Naso,* 6. *Labeo,* 7. *Bucco,* 8. *Strabo,* 9. *Obstipus,* 10, *Strumosus,* 11. *Gibbosus,* 12. *Loripes,* 13. *Cilo,* 15. adde *Calvastrum,* 14.

The Dressing of Gardens. - XLV. - Hortorum cultura.

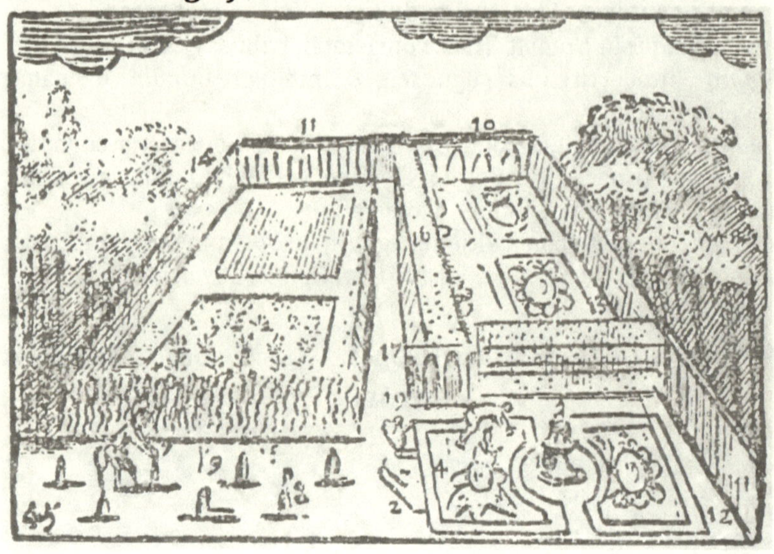

We have seen Man: Now let us go on to Man's *living,* and to *Handycraft-Trades,* which tend to it.

The first and most ancient *sustenance,* were the *Fruits of the Earth.*

Hereupon the first labour of Adam, was *the dressing of a garden.*

The *Gardener,* 1. diggeth in a *Garden-plot,* with a *Spade,* 2. or *Mattock,* 3. and maketh *Beds,* 4. and places wherein to plant *Trees,* 5. on which he setteth *Seeds* and *Plants.*

The *Tree-Gardener,* 6. planteth Trees, 7. in an *Orchard,* and grafteth *Cyons,* 8, in *Stocks,* 9.

He fenceth his Garden, either by care, with a *mound,* 10. or a *Stone-wall,* 11. or a *rail,* 12. or *Pales,* 13. or a *Hedge,* 14. made of *Hedge-stakes,* and *bindings;*

Or by Nature, with *Brambles* and *Bryers,* 15.

It is beautified with *Walks.* 16. and *Galleries,* 17.

It is watered with *Fountains,* 18. and a *Watering-pot,* 19.

Vidimus hominem: Jam pergamus ad *Victum* hominis, & ad *Artes Mechanicas,* quae huc faciunt.

Primus & antiquissimus *Victus,* erant *Fruges Terrae.*

Hinc primus Labor Adami, *Horti cultura.*

Hortulanus (Olitor), 1. fodit in *Viridario, Ligone,* 2. aut *Bipalio,* 3. facitque *Pulvinos,* 4. ac *Plantaria,* 5. quibus inserit *Semina* & *Plantas. Arborator,* 6. plantat Arbores, 7. in *Pomtario, inseritque Surculos,* 8. *Viviradicibus,* 9.

Sepit hortum vel Cura, *Muro,* 10. aut *Macerie,* 11. aut *Vacerra,* 12. aut *Plancis,* 13. aut *Sepe,* 14. *flexâ è sudibus* & *vitilibus;*

Vel Natura *Dumis* & *Vepribus,* 15. Ornatur *Ambulacris,* 16. & *Pergulis,* 17. Rigatur *Fontanis,* 18. & *Harpagio,* 19.

Husbandry. - XLVI. - Agricultura.

The *Plow-man,* 1. yoketh *Oxen,* 3. to a *Plough,* 2. and holding the *Plowstilt,* 4. in his left hand, and the *Plow-staff,* 5. in his right hand, with which he removeth *Clods,* 6. he cutteth the Land, (which was manured afore with *Dung,* 8.) with a *Share,* 7. and a *Coulter,* and maketh *furrows,* 9.

Then he *soweth* the *Seed,* 10. and harroweth it in with a *Harrow,* 11.

The *Reaper,* 12. sheareth the ripe corn with a *Sickle,* 13.gathereth up the *handfuls,* 14. and bindeth the *Sheaves.* 15.

The *Thrasher,* 16. thrasheth Corn on the *Barnfloor,* 17. with a *Flayl,* 18. tosseth it in a *winnowing-basket,* 19. and so when the *Chaff,* and the *Straw,* 20. are separated from it, he putteth it into *Sacks,* 12.

The *Mower,* 22. maketh *Hay* in a *Meadow,* cutting, down *Grass* with a *Sithe,* 23. and raketh it together with a *Rake,* 24. and maketh up *Cocks,* 26. with a *fork,* 25, and carrieth it on *Carriages,* 27. into the *Hay-barn,* 28.

Arator, 1. jungit *Boves,* 3. *Aratro,* 2. & tenens *Stivam,* 4. laevâ, *Rallum,* 5. dextrâ, quâ amovet *Glebas,* 6. scindit terram (stercoratam antea *Fimo,* 8.) *Vomere,* 7. et *Dentali,* facitque *Sulcos,* 9. Tum *seminat Semen,* 10. & inoccat *Occâ,* 11.

Messor, 12. metit fruges maturas *Falce messoris,* 13. colligit *Manipulos,* 14. & colligat *Mergetes,* 15. *Tritor,* 16. triturat frumentum in *Area Horrei,* 17. *Flagello* (tribula), 18. jactat *ventilabro,* 19. atque ita *Paleâ* & *Stramine,* 20. separatâ, congerit in *Saccos,* 21.

Foeniseca, 22, facit *Foenum* in *Prato,* desecans *Gramen Falce foenaria,* 23. corraditque *Rastro,* 24. componit *Acervos,* 26. *Furca,* 25. & convehit *Vehibus,* 27. in *Foenile,* 28.

Grasing. - XLVII. - Pecuaria.

Tillage of ground, and *keeping Cattle,* was in old time the care of Kings and Noble-men; at this Day only of the meanest sort of People.

The *Neat-heard,* 1. calleth out the *Heards,* 2. out of the *Beast-houses,* 3. with a *Horn,* 4. and driveth them to feed.

The *Shepherd,* 5. feedeth his *Flock,* 6. being furnished with a *Pipe,* 7. and a *Scrip,* 8. and a *Sheep-hook,* 9. having with him a great *Dog,* 10. fenced with a *Collar,* 11. against the *Wolves.*

Swine, 12. are fed out of a *Swine-Trough.*

The *Farmer's Wife,* 13. milketh the *Udders* of the *Cow,* 15. at the *Cratch,* 15. over a *milk-pale,* 16. and maketh *Butter* of *Cream* in a *Churn,* 17. and *Cheeses,* 18. of *Curds.*

The *Wool,* 19. is shorn from *Sheep,* whereof several *Garments* are made.

Cultus Agrorum, & *res pecuaria,* antiquissimis temporibus, erat cura Regum, Heroum; hodie tantum infirmae Plebis,

Bubulcus, 1. evocat *Armenia,* 2. è *Bovilibus,* 3. *Buccina* (Cornu), 4, & ducit pastum.

Opilio (Pastor), 5. pascit *Gregem,* 6. instructus *Fistula,* 7. & *Pera,* 8. ut & *Pedo,* 9. habens secum *Molossum,* 10. munitum *Millo,* 11. contra Lupos.

Sues, 12. saginantur ex *aqualiculo harae,*

Villica, 13. mulget *Ubera vaccae,* 14. ad *Praesepe,* 15. super *mulctra,* 16. et facit *Butyrum* è *flore lactis,* in *Vase butyraceo,* 17. et *Caseos,* 18. è *Coagulo.*

Lana, 19. detondetur *Ovibus,* ex quà variae *Vestes* conficiuntur.

The making of Honey. - XLVIII. – Mellificium.

The *Bees* send out a *swarm,* 1. and set over it a *Leader,* 2.

That swarm being ready to fly away is recalled by the Tinkling of a *brazen Vessel,* 3. and is put up into a new *Hive,* 4.

They make little *Cells* with six corners, 5. and fill them with *Honey-dew,* and make *Combs,* 6. out of which the *Honey* runneth, 7.

The *Partitions* being melted by fire, turn into *Wax,* 8.

Apes emittunt *Examen,* 1. adduntque illi *Ducem* (Regem), 2.

Examen illud, avolaturum, revocatur tinnitu *Vasis aenei,* 3. & includitur novo *Alveari,* 4.

Struunt *Cellulas* sexangulares, 5. et complent eas *Melligine,* & faciunt *Favos,* 6. è quibus *Mel* effluit, 7. *Crates* liquati igne abeunt in *Ceram,* 8.

Grinding. - XLIX. – Molitura.

In a *Mill,* 1. a Stone, 2. runneth upon a stone, 3.

A *Wheel,* 4. turning them about and grindeth Corn poured in by a *Hopper,* 5, and parteth the *Bran,* 6. falling into the *Trough,* 7. from the *Meal* slipping through a *Bolter,* 8.

Such a Mill was first a *Hand-mill,* 9. then a *Horse-mill,* 10. then a *Water-mill,* 11. then a *Ship-mill,* 12. and at last a *Wind-mill,* 13.

In *Mola,* Lapis, 2. currit super lapidem, 3. *Rota,* 4. circumagente, et conterit grana infusa per *Infundibulum,* 5. separatque *Furfurem,* 6. decidentem in *Cistam,* 7. à *Farina* (Polline) elabente per *Excussorium,* 7.

Talis Mola primùm fuit *Manuaria,* 9. deinde *Jumentaria,* 10. turn *Aquatica,* 11. & *Navalis,* 12. tandem, *Alata* (pneumatica), 13.

Bread-baking. - L. – Panificium.

The *Baker,* 1. sifteth the *Meal* in a *Rindge,* 2. and putteth it into the *Kneading-trough,* 3.

Then he poureth water to it and maketh *Dough,* 4. and kneadeth it with a *wooden slice,* 5.

Then he maketh *Loaves,* 6. *Cakes,* 7. *Cimnels,* 8. *Rolls,* 9, &c.

Afterwards he setteth them on a *Peel,* 10. and putteth them thorow the *Oven-mouth,* 12. into the *Oven,* 11.

But first he pulleth out the fire and the Coals with a *Coal-rake,* 13. which he layeth on a heap underneath, 14.

And thus is *Bread* baked, having the *Crust* without, 15, and the *Crumb* within, 16.

Pistor, 1. cernit *Farinam Cribo,* 2. (pollinario) & indit *Mactrae,* 3.
Tum affundit aquam, & facit *Massam,* 4. depsitque *spatha,* 5. ligneâ.
Dein format *Panes,* 6. *Placentas,* 7. *Similas,* 8. *Spiras,* 9. &c.
Post imponit *Palae,* 10. & ingerit *Furno,* 11. per *Praefurnium,* 12.
Sed priùs eruit ignem & Carbones *Rutabulo,* 13. quos congerit infra, 14.
Et sic *Panis* pinsitur habens extra *Crustam,* 15. intus *Micam,* 16.

Fishing. - LI. - Piscatio.

The *Fisher-man,* 1. catcheth fish, either on the Shoar, with an *Hook,* 2. which hangeth by a *Line* from the *angling-rod,* on which the *Bait* sticketh; or with a *Cleek-net,* 3. which hangeth on a *Pole,* 4. is put into the Water; or in a *Boat,* 5. with a *Trammel-net,* 6. or with a *Wheel,* 7. which is laid in the Water by Night.

Piscator, 1. captat pisces, sive in littore, *Hamo,* 2. qui pendet *filo* ab *arundine,* & cui *Esca* inhaeret; sive *Fundâ,* 3. quae pendens *Pertica,* 4, immittitur aquae; sive in *Cymba,* 5. Reti, 6. sive *Nassa,* 7. quae demergitur per Noctem.

Fowling. – LII. - Aucupium.

The *Fowler,* 1. maketh a *Bed,* 2, spreadeth a *Bird-net,* 3. throweth a *Bait,* 4. upon it, and hiding himself in a *Hut,* 5. he allureth Birds, by the chirping of *Lure-birds,* which partly hop upon the Bed, 6. and are partly shut in *Cages,* 7. and thus he entangleth Birds that fly over, in his net whilst they settle themselves down.

Or he setteth *Snares,* 8. on which they hang and strangle themselves:

Or setteth *Lime-twigs,* 9. on a *Perch,* 10. upon which if they sit they enwrap their Feathers, so that they cannot fly away, and fall down to the ground.

Or he catcheth them with a *Pole,* 11. or *a Pit-fall,* 12.

Auceps, 1. exstruit *Aream,* 2. superstruit illi *Rete* aucupatorium, 3. obsipat *Escam,* 4. & abdens se in *Latibulo,* 5. allicit Aves, cantu *Illicum,* qui partim in Area currunt, 6. partim inclusi sunt *Caveis,* 7. atque ita obruit transvolantes Aves Reti, dum se demittunt:

Aut tendit *Tendiculas,* 8. quibus suspendunt & suffocant seipsas:

Aut exponit *Viscatos calamos,* 9. *Amiti,* 10. quibus si insident, implicant pennas, ut nequeant avolare, & decidunt in terram.

Aut captat *Perficâ,* 11. vel *Decipulâ,* 12.

Hunting. - LIII. - Venatus.

The *Hunter,* 1. hunteth wild Beasts whilst he besetteth a Wood with *Toyls,* 2. stretched out upon *Shoars,* 3.

The *Beagle,* 4. tracketh the wild Beast or findeth him out by the scent; the *Tumbler,* or *Greyhound,* 5. pursueth it.

The *Wolf,* falleth in a *Pit,* 6. the *Stag,* 7. as he runneth away, into *Toyls.*

The *Boar,* 8. is struck through with a *Hunting-spear,* 9.

The *Bear,* 10. is bitten by Dogs, and is knocked with a *Club,* 11.

If any thing get away, it escapeth, 12. as here a *Hare* and a *Fox.*

Venator, 1. venatur Feras, dum cingit Sylvam, *Cassibus,* 2. tentis super *Varos,* 3. (furcillas.)

Canis sagax, 4. vestigat Feram, aut indagat odoratu; *Vertagus,* 5. persequitur. *Lupus,* incidit in *Foveam,* 6. fugiens *Cervus,* 7. in *Plagas.*

Aper, 8. transverberatur *Venabulo,* 9.

Ursus, 10. mordetur à Canibus, & tunditur *Clavâ,* 11.

Si quid effugit, evadit, 12. ut hic *Lepus* & *Vulpes.*

Butchery. - LIV. - Lanionia.

The *Butcher,* 1. killeth *fat Cattle,* 2. (The *Lean,* 3. are not fit to eat.)

He knocketh them down with an *Ax,* 4. or cutteth their Throat with a *Slaughter-knife,* 5. he flayeth them, 6. and cutteth them in pieces, and hangeth out the flesh to sell in the *Shambles,* 7.

He dresseth a *Swine,* 8. with fire or scalding water, 9. and maketh *Gamons,* 10. *Pistils,* 11. and *Flitches,* 12.

Besides several *Puddings, Chitterlings,* 13. *Bloodings,* 14. *Liverings,* 15. *Sausages,* 16. The *Fat,* 17. and *Tallow,* 18. are melted.

Lanio, 1. mactat *Pecudem altilem,* 2. (*Vescula,* 3. non sunt vescenda.)

Prosternit *Clavâ,* 4. vel jugulat.

Cunaculo, 5. excoriat (deglubit,) 6. dissecatque & exponit carnes, venum in *Macello,* 7.

Glabrat *Suem,* 8. igne, vel *aquâ fervidâ,* 9. & facit *Pernas,* 10. *Petasones,* 11. & *Succidias,* 12.

Prаetereà *Farcimina* varia, *Faliscos,* 13. *Apexabones,* 14. *Tomacula,* 15. *Botulos,* (Lucanicas) 16.

Adeps, 17. & *Sebum,* 18. eliquantur.

Cookery. - LV. – Coquinaria.

The Yeoman of the Larder, 1. bringeth forth *Provision,* 2. out of the *Larder,* 3. The *Cook,* 4. taketh them and maketh *several Meats.*

He first pulleth off the Feathers and draweth the Gutts out of the *Birds,* 5.

He scaleth and splitteth *Fish,* 6.

He draweth some flesh with *Lard,* by means of a *Larding-needle,* 7,

He caseth *Hares,* 8. then he boileth them in *Pots,* 9. and *Kettles,* 10. on the *Hearth,* 11. and scummeth them with a *Scummer,* 12.

He seasoneth things that are boyled with Spices, which he poundeth with a *Pestil,* 14. in a *Morter,* 13. Or grateth with a *Grater,* 15.

He roasteth some on *Spits,* 16. and with a *Jack,* 17. or upon a *Grid-iron,* 18.

Or fryeth them in a *Frying-pan,* 19. upon a *Brand-iron,* 20.

Kitchen utensils besides are, a *Coal-rake,* 21. a *Chafing-dish,* 22. a *Trey,* 23. (in which *Dishes,* 24. and *Platters,* 25. are washed), a pair of *Tongs,* 26. a *Shredding-knife,* 27. a *Colander,* 28. a *Basket,* 29. and a *Besom,* 30.

Promus Condus, 1. profert *Obsonia,* 2, è *Penu,* 3. *Coquus,* 4. accipit ea & coquit *varia Esculenta.* Prius deplumat, & exenterat *Aves,* 5. Desquamat & exdorsuat *Pisces,* 6. Trajectat quasdem carnes *Lardo,* ope *Creacentri,* 7.

Lepores, 8. exuit, tum elixat *Ollis,* 9. & *Cacabis,* 10. in *Foco,* 11. & despumat *Lingula,* 12. Condit elixata, Aromatibus, quae comminuit *Pistillo,* 14. in *Mortario,* 13. aut terit *Radulâ,* 15.

Quaedam assat *Verubus,* 16. & *Automato,* 17. vel super *Craticulum,* 18. Vel frigit *Sartagine,* 19. super *Tripodem,* 20.

Vasa Coquinaria praeterea sunt, *Rutabulum,* 21. *Foculus* (Ignitabulum), 22. *Trua,* 23. (in quà *Catini,* 24. & *Patinae,* 25. eluuntur) *Forceps,* 26. *Culter incisorius,* 27. *Qualus,* 28. *Corbis,* 29. & *Scopa,* 30.

The Vintage. - LVI. - Vindemia.

Wine groweth in the *Vine-yard,* 1. where *Vines* are propagated and tyed with Twigs to *Trees,* 2. or to *Props,* 3. or *Frames,* 4.

When the time of Grape-gathering is come, they cut off the *Bunches,* and carry them in *Measures of three Bushels,* 5. and throw them into a *Vat,* 6. and tread them with their *Feet,* 7. or stamp them with a *Wooden-Pestil,* 8. and squeeze out the juice in a *Wine-press,* 9. which is called *Must,* 11. and being received in a great *Tub,* 10. it is poured into *Hogsheads,* 12. it is stopped up, 15. and being laid close in *Cellars* upon *Settles,* 14. it becometh *Wine.*

It is drawn out of the *Hogshead,* with a *Cock,* 13. or *Faucet,* 16. (in which is a *Spigot*) the Vessel being unbunged.

Vinum crescit in *Vinea,* 1. ubi *Vites* propagantur, & alligantur viminibus ad *Arbores,* 2. vel ad *Palos* (ridicas), 3. vel ad *Juga,* 4

Cum tempus vindemiandi adest, abscindunt *Botros,* & comportant *Trimodiis,* 5. conjiciuntque in *Lacum,* 6. calcant *Pedibus.* 7. aut tundunt *Ligneo Pilo,* 8. & exprimunt succum *Torculari,* 9. qui dicitur *Mustum,* 11. & exceptum *Orcâ,* 10. infunditur *Vasis* (Doliis), 12. operculatur, 15. & abditum in *Cellis,* super *Cantherios,* 14. abit in *Vinum.*

Promitur e *Dolio Siphone,* 13. aut *Tubulo,* 16. (in quo est *Epistomium*) Vase relito.

Brewing. - LVII. - Zythopoie.

Where *Wine* is not to be had they drink *Beer,* which is brewed of *Malt,* 1 . and *Hops,* 2. in a *Caldron,* 3. afterwards it is poured into *Vats,* 4. and when it is cold, it is carried in *Soes,* 5, into the *Cellar,* 6. and is put into *Vessels.*

Brandy-wine, extracted by the power of heat from dregs of Wine in a *Pan,* 7. over which a *Limbeck,* 8. is placed, droppeth through a *Pipe,* 9. into a *Glass.*

Wine and Beer when they turn sowre, become *Vinegar.* Of Wine and Honey they make *Mead.*

Ubi *Vinum* non habetur, bibitur *Cerevisia* (Zythus), quae coquitur ex *Byne,* 1. & *Lupulo,* 2. in *Aheno,* 3. post effunditur in *Lacus,* 4. & frigefactum, defertur *Labris,* 5. in *Cellaria,* 6. & intunditur vasibus.

Vinum sublimatum, extractum vi Caloris e fecibus Vini in *Aheno,* 7. cui *Alembicum,* 8. superimpositum est. destillat per *Tubum,* 9. in *Vitrum.* Vinum & Cerevisia, cum acescunt, fiunt *Acetum.* Ex Vino & Melle faciunt *Mulsum.*

A Feast. - LVIII. - Convivium.

When a *Feast* is made ready, the table is covered with a *Carpet,* 1. and a *Table-cloth,* 2. by the *Waiters,* who besides lay the *Trenchers,* 3. *Spoons,* 4. *Knives,* 5. with little *Forks,* 6. *Table-napkins,* 7. *Bread,* 8. with a *Salt-seller,* 9.

Messes are brought in *Platters,* 10. a *Pie,* 19. on a *Plate.*

The Guests being brought in by the *Host,* 11. wash their Hands out of a *Laver, 12.* or *Ewer,* 14. over a *Hand-basin,* 13. or *Bowl,* 15. and wipe them on a *Hand-towel,* 16. then they sit at the Table on *Chairs,* 17.

The *Carver,* 18. breaketh up the good Cheer, and divideth it.

Sauces are set amongst *Roast-meat,* in Sawcers, 20.

The *Butler,* 21. filleth *strong Wine* out of a *Cruise,* 25. or *Wine-pot,* 26. or *Flagon,* 27. into *Cups,* 22. or *Glasses,* 23. which stand on a *Cupboard,* 24. and he reacheth them to the *Master of the Feast,* 28. who drinketh to his *Guests.*

Cum *Convivium* apparatur, Mensa sternitur *Tapetibus,* 1. & *Mappa,* 2. a *Tricliniariis,* qui praetereà opponunt *Discos* (Orbes), 3. *Cochlearia,* 4. *Cultros,* 5. cum *Fuscinulis,* 6. *Mappulas,* 7. *Panem,* 8. cum *Salino,* 9. *Fercula* inferuntur in *Patinis,* 10. *Artocrea,* 19. in *Lance.*

Convivae introducti ab *Hospite,* 11. abluunt manus è *Gutturnio,* 12. vel *Aquali,* 14. super *Malluvium,* 13. aut *Pelvim,* 15. terguntque *Mantili,* 16. tum assident Mensae per *Sedilia,* 17.

Structor, 18. deartuat dapes, & distribuit.

Embammata interponuntur *Assutaris* in Scutellis, 20. *Pincerna,* 21. infundit *Temetum,* ex *Urceo,* 25. vel *Cantharo,* 26. vel *Lagena,* 27. in *Pocula,* 22. vel *Vitrea,* 23. quae extant in *abaco,* 24. & porrigit, *Convivatori,* 28. qui propinat *Hospitibus.*

The Dressing of Line. - LXIX. - Tractatio Lini.

Line and *Hemp* being rated in water, and dryed again, 1. are braked with a *wooden Brake,* 2. where the *Shives,* 3. fall down, then they are heckled with an *Iron Heckle,* 4. where the *Tow,* 5. is parted from it.

Flax is tyed to a *Distaff,* 6. by the *Spinster,* 7, which with her left hand pulleth out the *Thread,* 8. and with her right hand turneth a *Wheel,* 9. or a *Spindle,* 10. upon which is a *Wharl,* 11.

The *Spool* receiveth the *Thread,* 13. which is drawn thence upon a *Yarn-windle,* 14. hence either *Clews,* 15. are wound up, or *Hanks,* 16. are made.

Linum & Cannabis, macerata aquis, et siccata rursum, 1. contunduntur *Frangibulo ligneo,* 2. ubi *Cortices,* 3. decidunt tum carminantur *Carmine ferreo,* 4. ubi *Stupa,* 5. separatur.

Linum purum alligatur *Colo,* 6. à *Netrice,* 7. quae sinistra trahit *Filum,* 8. dexterâ, 12.

Rhombum (girgillum), 9. vel *Fusum,* 10. in quo *Verticillus,* 11. *Volva* accipit *Fila,* 13. inde deducuntur in *Alabrum,* 14. hinc vel *Glomi,* 15. glomerantur, vel *Fasciculi,* 16. fiunt.

Weaving. - LX. - Textura.

The *Webster* undoeth the *Clews,* 1. into *Warp,* and wrappeth it about the *Beam,* 2. and as he sitteth in his *Loom,* 3. he treadeth upon the *Treddles,* 4. with his Feet.

He divideth the *Warp,* 5. with *Yarn,* and throweth the *Shuttle,* 6. through, in which is the *Woofe,* and striketh it close. with the *Sley,* 7. and so maketh *Linen cloth,* 8.

So also the *Clothier* maketh *Cloth* of *Wool.*

Textor diducit *Glomos,* 1. in *Stamen,* & circumvolvit *Jugo,* 2. ac sedens in *Textrino,* 3. calcat *Insilia,* 4. pedibus.

Diducit *Stamen,* 5. *Liciis,* & trajicit *Radium,* 6. in quo est *Trama,* ac densat. *Pectine,* 7. atque ita conficit *Linteum,* 8. Sic etiam *Pannifex facit Pannum è Lana.*

Linen Cloths. - LXI. - Lintea.

Linnen-webs are bleached in the *Sun,* 1. with Water poured on them, 2. till they be white.

Of them the *Sempster,* 3. soweth *Shirts,* 4. *Handkirchers,* 5. *Bands,* 6. *Caps,* &c.

These if they be fouled, are washed again by the *Laundress,* 7. in water, or *Lye* and *Sope.*

Linteamina insolantur, 1. aquâ perfusâ, 2. donec candefiant.

Ex iis *Sartrix,* 3. suit *Indusia,* 4. *Muccinia,* 5. *Collaria,* 6. *Capitia,* &c.

Haec, si sordidentur lavantur rursum, a *Lotrice,* 7. aquâ, sive *Lixivio* ac *Sapone.*

The Taylor. - LXII. - Sartor.

The *Taylor,* 1. cutteth *Cloth,* 2. with *Shears,* 3. and seweth it together with a *Needle* and *double thread,* 4.

Then he presseth the *Seams* with a *Pressing-iron,* 5. And thus he maketh *Coats,* 6. with *Plaits,* 7. in which the *Border,* 8. is below with *Laces,* 9. *Cloaks,* 10. with a *Cape,* 11. and *Sleeve Coats,* 12. *Doublets,* 13. with *Buttons,* 14. and *Cuffs,* 15. *Breeches,* 16. sometimes with *Ribbons,* 17. *Stockins,* 18. *Gloves,* 19. *Muntero Caps,* 20. &c. So the *Furrier* maketh *Furred Garments* of *Furs.*

Sartor, 1. discindit *Pannum,* 2. *Forfice,* 3, consuitque *Acu* & *Filo duplicato,* 4. Posteâ complanat *Suturas Ferramento,* 5. Sicque conficit *Tunicas,* 6. *Plicatas,* 7. in quibus infra est *Fimbria,* 8. cum *Institis,* 9. *Pallia,* 10. cum *Patagio,* 11. & *Togas Manicatas,* 12. *Thoraces,* 13. cum *Globulis,* 14. & *Manicis,* 15. *Caligas,* 16. aliquando cum *Lemniscis,* 17. *Tibialia,* 18. *Chirothecas,* 19. *Amiculum,* 20. &c. Sic *Pellio* facit *Pellicia* è *Pellibus.*

The Shoemaker. - LXIII. - Sutor.

The *Shoemaker,* 1. maketh *Slippers,* 7. *Shoes,* 8. (in which is seen above, the *Upper-leather,* beneath the *Sole,* and on both sides the *Latchets*) *Boots,* 9. and *High Shoes,* 10. of *Leather,* 5. (which is cut with a *Cutting-knife*), 6. by means of an *Awl,* 2. and *Lingel,* 3. upon a *Last,* 4.

Sutor, 1. conficit *Crepidas* (Sandalia,) 7. *Calceos,* 8. (in quibus spectator superne *Obstragulum,* inferne *Solea,* et utrinque *Ansae*)
Ocreas, 9. et *Perones,* 10. e *Corio,* 5. (quod discinditur *Scalpro Sutorio,* 6.) ope *Subulae,* 2. et Fili *picati,* 3. super *Modum,* 4.

The Carpenter. - LXIV. - Faber lignarius.

We have seen Man's food and clothing: now his Dwelling followeth.

At first they dwelt in *Caves,* 1. then in *Booths* or *Huts,* 2. And then again in *Tents,* 3. at the last in *Houses.*

The *Woodman* felleth and heweth down *Trees,* 5. with an *Ax,* 4. the *Boughs,* 6. remaining.

He cleaveth *Knotty Wood* with a *Wedge,* 7. which he forceth in with a *Beetle,* 8. and maketh *Wood-stacks,* 9.

The *Carpenter* squareth *Timber* with a *Chip-Ax,* 10. whence *Chips,* 11. fall, and saweth it with a *Saw,* 12. where the *Saw-dust,* 13. falleth down.

Afterwards he lifteth the *Beam* upon *Tressels,* 14. by the help of a *Pully,* 15. fasteneth it with *Cramp-irons,* 16. and marketh it out with a *Line,* 17. Thus he frameth the *Walls* together, 18. and fasteneth the great pieces with *Pins,* 19.

Hominis victum & amictum, vidimus: sequitur nunc Domicilium ejus.

Primò habitabant in *Specubus,* 1. deinde in *Tabernaculis* vel *Tuguriis,* 2. tum etiam in *Tentoriis,* 3. demum in *Domibus.*

Lignator sternit & truncat *Arbores,* 5. *Securi,* 4. remanentibus *Sarmentis,* 6.

Findit *Nodosum, Lignum Cuneo,* 7. quem adigit *Tudite,* 8. & componit *Strues,* 9.

Faber Lignarius ascit *Ascia,* 10. *Materiem,* unde *Assulae,* 11. cadunt, & serrat *Serrâ,* 12. ubi *Scobs,* 13. decidit.

Post elevat *Tignum* super *Canterios,* 14. ope *Trochleae,* 15. affigit *Ansis,* 16. & lineat *Amussi,* 17. Tum compaginat *Parietes,* 18. & configit trabes *Clavis trabalibus,* 19.

The Mason. - LXV. - Faber Murarius,

The *Mason,* 1. layeth a *Foundation,* and buildeth *Walls,* 2.

Either of *Stones* which the *Stone-digger* getteth out of the *Quarry,* 3. and the *Stone-cutter,* 4. squareth by a *Rule,* 5.

Or of *Bricks,* 6. which are made of *Sand* and *Clay* steeped in water, and are burned in fire.

Afterwards he plaistereth it with *Lime,* by means of a *Trowel,* and garnisheth witli a *Rough-cast,* 8.

Faber Murarius, 1. ponit *Fundamentum,* & struit *Muros,* 2.

Sive è *Lapidibus,* quos *Lapidarius* eruit in *Lapicidina,* 3. & *Latomus,* 4. conquadrat ad *Normam,* 5.

Sive è *Lateribus,* 6, qui formantur, ex *Arena* & *Luto,* aquâ intritis & excoquuntur igne.

Dein crustat *Calce,* ope *Trullae,* 7. & vestit *Tectorio,* 8.

Engines - LXVI. - Machinae.

One can carry as much by thrusting a *Wheel-barrow,* 3. before him, (having an *Harness,* 4. hanging on his neck,) as two men can carry on a *Colestaff,* 1. or *Hand-barrow,* 2. But he can do more that rolleth a Weight laid upon *Rollers,* 6. with a *Leaver,* 5.

A *Wind-beam,* 7. is a post, which is turned by going about it.

A *Crane,* 8. hath a *Hollow-wheel,* in which one walking draweth weights out of a Ship, or letteth them down into a Ship.

A *Rammer,* 9. is used to fasten *Piles,* 10. it is lifted with a Rope drawn by *Pullies,* 11. or with hands, if it have *handles,* 12.

Unus potest ferre tantum trudendo *Pabonem,* 3. ante se, (*Aerumna,* Suspensâ a Collo) quantum duo possunt ferre Palangâ, vel Feretro, 2.

Plus autem potest qui provolvit Molem impositam *Phalangis* (Cylindris, 6.) *Vecte,* 5. *Ergata,* 7. est columella, quae versatur circumeundo.

Geranium, 8. habet *Tympanum,* cui inambulans quis extrahit pondera navi, aut demittit in navem.

Fistuca, 9. adhibetur ad pangendum *Sublicas,* 10. adtollitur Fune tracto per *Trochleas,* 11. vel manibus, si habet *ansas,* 12.

A House. - LXVII. - Domus.

The *Porch,* 1. is before the *Door* of the *House.* The *Door* hath a *Threshold,* 2. and a *Lintel,* 3. and *Posts,* 4. on both sides.

The *Hinges,* 5. are upon the right hand, upon which the *Doors,* 6. hang, the *Latch,* 7. and the *Bolt,* 8. are on the left hand.

Before the House is a *Fore-court,* 9. with a *Pavement* of *square stones,* 10. born up with *Pillars,* 11. in which is the *Chapiter,* 1 2. and the *Base,* 13.

They go up into the upper Stories by *Greess,* 14. and *Winding-stairs,* 15.

The *Windows,* 16. appear on the outside, and the *Grates,* 17. the *Galleries,* 18. the *Watertables,* 19. the *Butteresses,* 20. to bear up the walls.

On the top is the *Roof,* 21. covered with *Tyles,* 22. or *Shingles,* 23. which lie upon *Laths,* 24. and these upon *Rafters,* 25.

The *Eaves,* 26. adhere to the *Roof.*

The place without a Roof is called an *open Gallery,* 27.

In the Roof are *Jettings out,* 28, and *Pinnacles,* 29.

Vestibulum, 1. est ante *Januam Domûs.*

Janua habet *Limen,* 2. & *Superliminare,* 3. & *Postes,* 4. utrinque.

Cardines, 5. sunt a dextris, à quibus pendent *Fores,* 6. *Claustrum,* 7. aut *Pessulus,* 8. a sinistris.

Sub aedibus est *Cavaedium,* 9. *Pavimento Tessellato,* 10. fulcitum *Columnis,* 11. in quibus *Peristylium,* 12. & *Basis,* 13.

Ascenditur in superiores contignationes per *Scalas,* 14. & *Cocklidia,* 15.

Fenestrae, 16. apparent extrinsecus, & *Cancelli* (clathra), 17. *Pergulae,* 18. *Suggrundia,* 19. & *Fulcra,* 20. fulciendis muris.

In summo est *Tectum,* 21. contectum *Imbricibus* (*tegulis*), 22. vel *Scandulis,* 23. quae incumbunt *Tigillis,* 24. haec *Tignis,* 25.

Tecto adhaeret *Stillicidium,* 26.

Locus sine Tecto dicitur *Subdiale,* 27.

In Tecto sunt *Meniana,* 28. & *Coronides,* 29.

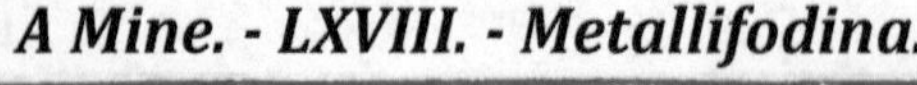

A Mine. - LXVIII. - Metallifodina.

Miners, 1. go into the *Grave,* 2. by a *Stick,* 3. or by *Ladders,* 4. with *Lanthorns,* 5. and dig out with a *Pick,* 6. the *Oar,* which being put in *Baskets,* 7. is drawn out with a *Rope,* 8. by means of a *Turn,* 9. and is carried to the *Melting-house,* 10. where it is forced with *fire,* that the *Metal* may run out, 12. the *Dross,* 11. is thrown aside.

Metalli fossores, 1. ingrediuntur *Puteum fodinae,* 2. *Bacillo,* 3, sive *Gradibus,* 4. cum *Lucernis,* 5. & effodiunt *Ligone,* 6. *terram Metallicam,* quae imposita *Corbibus,* 7. extrahitur *Fune,* 8. ope *Machinae tractoriae,* 9. & defertur in *Ustrinam,* 10. ubi urgetur igne, ut *Metallum,* 12. profluat *Scoriae,* 11. abjiciuntur scorsim.

The Blacksmith. - LXIX. - Faber Ferrarius.

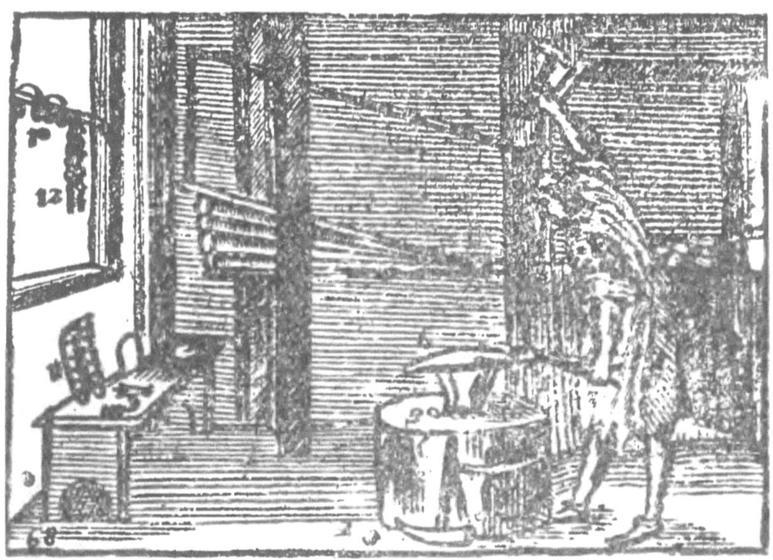

The *Blacksmith,* 1. in his *Smithy* (or Forge), 2. bloweth the fire with a *pair of Bellows,* 3. which he bloweth with his *Feet,* 4. and so heateth the *Iron:*

And then he taketh it out with the *Tongs,* 5. layeth it upon the *Anvile,* 6. and striketh it with an *Hammer,* 7. where the *sparks,* 8. fly off.

And thus are hammer'd out, *Nails,* 9. *Horse-shoes,* 10. *Cart-strakes,* 11. *Chains,* 12. *Plates, Locks* and *Keys, Hinges,* &c.

He quencheth hot Irons in a *Cool-trough.*

Faber ferrarius, 1. in *Ustrina* (Fabricâ), 2. inflat ignem *Folle,* 3. quem adtollit *Pede,* 4. atq; ita candefacit *Ferrum:*

Deinde eximit *Forcipe,* 5. imponit *Incudi,* 6. & cudit *Malleo,* 7. ubi *Stricturae,* 8. exiliunt.

Et sic excuduntur, *Clavi,* 9. *Solea,* 10. *Canthi,* 11. *Catenae,* 12. *Laminae, Serae* cum *Clavibus, Cardines,* &c.

Restinguit cadentia, Ferramenta in Lacti.

The Box-maker and the Turner. - LXX. - Scrinarius & Tornator.

The *Box-maker,* 1. smootheth *hewen Boards,* 2. with a *Plain,* 3. upon a *work-board, 4.* he maketh them very smooth with a *little-plain,* 5 . he boreth them thorow with an *Augre,* 6. carveth them with a *Knife,* 7. fasteneth them together with *Glew* and *Cramp-Irons,* 8. and maketh *Tables,* 9. *Boards,* 10. *Chests,* 11. &c.

The *Turner,* 12. sitting over the *Treddle,* 13. turneth with a *Throw,* 15. upon a *Turner's Bench,* 14. *Bowls,* 16. *Tops,* 17, *Puppets,* 18. and such like *Turners Work.*

Arcularius, 1. edolat *Asseres,* 2. *Runcina,* 3. in *Tabula,* 4. deplanat *Planula,* 5. perforat (terebrat) *Terebra,* 6. sculpit *Cultro,* 7. combinat *Glutine* & *Subscudibus,* 8. & facit *Tabulas,* 9. *Mensas,* 10. *Arcus* (Cistas), 11. &c.

Tornio, 12. sedens in *Insili,* 13. torn at *Torno,* 15. super *Scamno Tornatorio,* 14. *Globos,* 16. *Conos,* 17. *Icunculas,* 18, & similia *Toreumata.*

The Potter. - LXXI. - Figulus.

The *Potter,* 1. sitting over a *Wheel,* 2. maketh *Pots,* 4. *Pitchers,* 5. *Pipkins,* 6. *Platters,* 7. *Pudding-pans,* 8. *Juggs,* 9. *Lids,* 10. &c. of *Potter's Clay,* 3. afterwards he baketh them in an *Oven,* 11. and glazeth them with *White Lead,*

A broken Pot affordeth Pot-sheards, 12.

Figulas, 1. sedens super *Rota,* 2. format *Ollas,* 4. *Urceos,* 5. *Tripodes,* 6. *Patinas,* 7. *Vasa testacea,* 8. *Fidelias,* 9. *Opercula,* 10. &c. ex *Argillâ,* 3. postea excoquit in *Furno,* 11. & incrustat *Lithargyro.*

Fracta Olla dat *Testas,* 12.

The Parts of a House – LXXI. - Partes Domus.

A *House* is divided into inner *Rooms,* such as are the *Entry,* 1. the *Stove,* 2. the *Kitchen,* 3. the *Buttery,* 4. the *Dining Room,* 5. the *Gallery,* 6. the *Bed Chamber,* 7. with a *Privy,* 8. made by it.

Baskets, 9. are of use for carrying things, and *Chests,* 10. (which are made fast with a *Key,* 11.) for keeping them.

Under the *Roof,* is the *Floor,* 12. In the *Yard,* 13. is a *Well,* 14. a *Stable,* 15. and a *Bath,* 16. Under the House is the *Cellar,* 17.

Domus distinguitur in *Conclavia,* ut sunt *Atrium,* 1. *Hypocaustum,* 2. *Cella Penuaria,* 4. *Coenaculum,* 5. *Camera,* 6. *Cubiculum,* 7. cum *Secessu* (Latrina), 8. adstructo.

Corbes, 9. inserviunt rebus transferendis, Arcae, 10. (quae *Clavá,* 11. recluduntur) adfervandis illis.

Sub *Tecto,* est *Solum* (Pavimentum), 12. In *Area,* 13. *Puteus,* 14. *Stabulum,* 15. cum *Balneo,* 16. Sub Domo est *Cella,* 17.

The Stove with the Bed-room. - LXXIII. – Hypocaustum cum Dormitorio.

The *Stove,* 1. is beautified with an *Arched Roof*, 2. ,and *wainscoted Walls,* 3. It is enlightened with *Windows,* 4. It is heated with an *Oven,* 5.

Its Utensils are *Benches,* 6. *Stools,* 7. *Tables,* 8. with *Tressels,* 9. *Footstools,* 10. and *Cushions,* 11. There are also *Tapestries* hanged, 12.

For soft lodging in a *Sleeping-room,* 13. there is a *Bed,* 14. spread on a *Bedsted,* 15. upon a *Straw-pad,* 16. with *Sheets,* 17. and *Cover-lids,* 18.

The *Bolster,* 19. is under ones head.

The Bed is covered with a *Canopy,* 20.

A *Chamber-pot,* 21. is for making water in.

Hypocaustum, 1. ornatur *Laqueari,* 2. & *tabulatis Parietibus,* 3, Illuminatur *Fenestris,* 4. Calefit *Fornace,* 5.

Ejus Utensilia sunt *Scamna,* 6. *Sellae,* 7. *Mensae,* 8. cum *Fulcris,* 9. ac *Scabellis,* 10. & *Culcitris,* 11.

Appenduntur etiam *Tapetes,* 12.

Pro levi cubatu, in *Dormitorio,* 13. est *Lectus,* (Cubile) 14. stratus in *Sponda,* 15. super *Stramentum,* 16. cum *Lodicibus,* 17. & *Stragulis,* 18.

Cervical, 19. est sub capite. *Canopeo,* 20. *Lectus* tegitur.

Matula, 21. est vesicae levandae.

Wells. - LXXIV. - Putei.

Where *Springs* are wanting, *Wells,* 1. are digged. and they are compassed about with a *Brandrith,* 2. lest any one fall in.

Thence is water drawn with *Buckets,* 3. hanging either at a *Pole,* 4. or a *Rope,* 5. or a *Chain,* 6. and that either by a *Swipe,* 7. or a *Windle,* 8. or a *Turn,* 9. with a *Handle* or a *Wheel,* 10. or to conclude, by a *Pump,* 11.

Ubi *Fontes* deficiunt, *Putei,* 1. effodiuntur, & circumdantur *Crepidine,* 2. ne quis incidat.

Inde aqua hauritur *Urnis* (situlis), 3. pendentibus vel *Pertica,* 4. vel *Fune,* 5. vel *Catena,* 6. idque aut *Tollenone,* 7. aut *Girgillo,* 8. aut *Cylindro,* 9. *Manubriato.* aut *Rota* (tympano), 10. aut deinque *Antliâ,* 11.

The Bath. - LXXV. - Balneum.

He that desireth to be wash'd in cold water, goeth down into a *River,* 1.

In a *Bathing-house,* 2. we wash off the *filth* either sitting in a *Tub,* 3 or going up into the *Hot-house,* 4. and we are rubbed with a *Pumice-stone,* 6. or a *Hair-cloth,* 5.

In the *Stripping-room,* 7. we put off our clothes, and are tyed about with an *Apron,* 8.

We cover our Head with a *Cap,* 9. and put our feet into a *Bason,* 10.

The *Bath-woman,* 11. reacheth water in a *Bucket,* 12. drawn out of the *Trough,* 13. into which it runneth out of *Pipes,* 14.

The *Bath-keeper,* 15. lanceth with a *Lancet,* 16. and by applying *Cupping-glasses,* 17. he draweth the *Blood* betwixt the skin and the flesh, which he wipeth away with a *Spunge,* 18.

Qui cupit lavari aquâ frigidâ, descendit in *Fluvium,* 1.

In *Balneario,* 2. abluimus *squalores,* sive sedentes in *Labro,* 3. sive conscendentes in *Sudatorium,* 4. & defricamur *Pumice,* 6. aut *Cilicio,* 5.

In *Apodyterio,* 7. exuimus Vestes, & praecingimur *Castula* (Subligari), 8.

Tegimus caput *Pileolo,* 9. & imponimus pedes *Telluvio,* 10.

Balneatrix, 11. ministrat aquam *Situla,* 12. haustam ex *Alveo,* 13. in quem defluit è *Canalibus,* 14.

Balneator, 15. scarificat *Scalpro,* 16. & applicando *Cucurbitas,* 17. extrahit *Sanguinem* subcutaneum, quem abstergit *Spongiâ,* 18.

The Barbers Shop. - LXXVI. - Tonstrina.

The *Barber,* 1. in the *Barbers-shop,* 2, cutteth off the *Hair* and the *Beard* with a pair of *Sizzars,* 3. or shaveth with a *Razor,* which he taketh out of his *Case.*

And he washeth one over a *Bason,* 5. with *Suds* running out of a *Laver,* 6. and also with *Sope,* 7. and wipeth him with a *Towel,* 8. combeth him with a *Comb,* 9. and curleth him with a *Crisping Iron,* 10.

Sometimes he cutteth a *Vein* with a *Pen-knife,* 11. where the Blood spirteth out, 12. The *Chirurgeon* cureth *Wounds.*

Tonsor, 1. in *Tonstrina,* 2. tondet *Crines* & *Barbam Forcipe,* 3. vel radit *Novaculâ,* quam depromit è *Theca,* 4.

Et lavat super *Pelvim,* 5. *Lixivio* defluente è *Gulturnio,* 6. ut & *Sapone,* 7. & tergit *Linteo,* 8. pectit *Pectine,* 9. crispat *Calamistro,* 10.

Interdum secat Venam, *Scalpello,* 11. ubi Sanguis propullulat, 12. *Chirurgus* curat *Vulnera.*

The Stable. - LXXVII.

The *Horse-keeper,* 1. cleaneth the *Stable* from *Dung,* 2.

He tyeth a *Horse,* 3. with a *Halter,* 4. to the *Manger,* 5. or if he apt to bite, he maketh him fast with a *Muzzle,* 6.

Then he streweth *Litter,* 7. under him.

He *winnoweth Oats* with a *Van,* 8. (being mixt with Chaff, and taken out of a *Chest,* 10.) and with them feedeth the Horse, as also with *Hay,* 9.

Afterwards he leadeth him to the *Watering-trough,* 11. to water.

Then he rubbeth him with a *Cloth,* 12. combeth him with a *Curry-comb,* 15. covereth him with an *Housing-cloth,* 14. and looketh upon his *Hoofs* whether the *Shoes,* 13. be fast with the *Nails.*

Stabularias (Equiso), 1. purgat *Stabulum* a *Fimo,* 2 .

Alligat *Equum,* 3. *Capistro,* 4. ad *Praesepe,* 5. aut si mordax constringit *Fiscella,* 6.

Deinde substernit *Stramenta,* 7.

Ventilat Avenam, Vanno, 8.

(Paleis mixtam, ac depromptam à *Cista Pabulatoria,* 10.) câque pascit equum, ut & *Foeno,* 9. Postea ducit ad *Aquarium,* 11. aquatum.

Tum detergit *Panno,* 12. depectit *Strigili,* 15. insternit *Gausape,* 14. & inspicit *Soleas,* an *Calcei ferrei,* 13. firmis *Clavis* haereant.

Dials. - LXXVII. – Horologia.

A *Dial* measureth Hours.

A *Sun-dial,* 1. sheweth by the shadow of the *Pin,* 2. what a *Clock* it is; either on a Wall, or a *Compass,* 3,

An *Hour-glass,* 4. sheweth the four parts of an hour by the running of *Sand,* heretofore of water.

A *Clock,* 5. numbereth also the Hours of the Night, by the turning of the Wheels, the greatest whereof is drawn by a *Weight,* 6. and draweth the rest.

Then either the *Bell,* 7. by its sound, being struck on by the *Hammer,* or the *Hand,* 8. without, by its motion about sheweth the hour.

Horologium dimetitur Horas.

Solarium, 1. ostendit umbrâ *Gnomonis,* 2. quota sit *Hora;* sive in Pariete, sive in *Pyxide Magnetica,* 3.

Clepsydra, 4. ostendit partes horae quatuor, fluxu *Arenae,* olim aquae.

Automaton, 5. numerat etiam Nocturnas Horas, circulatione Rotarum, quarum maxima trahitur *à Pondere,* 6. trahit caeteras.

Tum vel *Campana,* 7. sonitu suo, percussa a *Malleolo,* vel *Index* extra Circuitione sua indicat horam.

The Picture. – LXXIX. - Pictura.

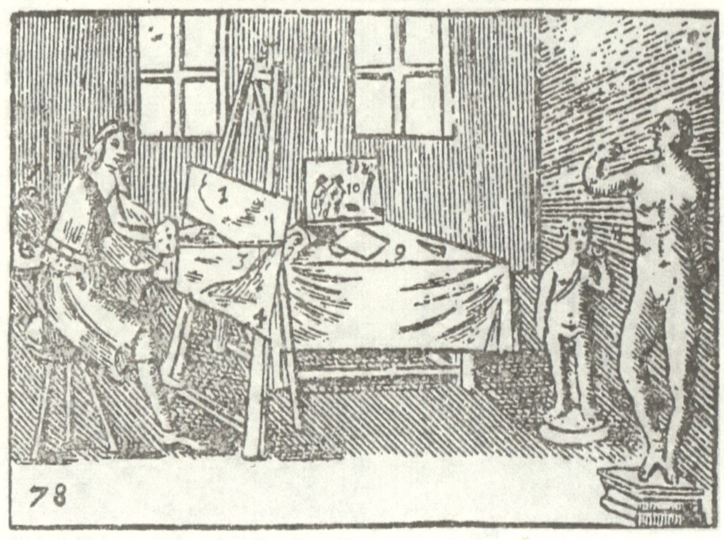

Pictures, 1 , delight the Eyes and adorn Rooms.

The *Painter,* 2. painteth an *Image* with a *Pencil,* 3. in a *Table,* 4. upon a *Case-frame,* 5. holding his *Pollet,* 6. in his left hand, on which are the *Paints* which were ground by the *Boy,* 7. on a *Marble.*

The *Carver,* and *Statuary* carve *Statues,* 8. of Wood and Stone. The *Graver* and the *Cutter* grave *Shapes,* 10. and *Characters* with a *Graving Chesil,* 9. in Wood, Brass, and other Metals.

Picturae, 1. oblectant Oculos & ornant Conclavia. *Pictor,* 2. pingit *Effigiem Penicilio,* 3. in *Tabula,* 4. super *Pluteo,* 5. tenens *Orbem Pictorium,* 6. in sinistra, in quo *Pigmenta* quae terebantur à *puero,* 7. in *marmore. Sculptor,* & *Statuarius* exsculpunt *Statuas,* 8. è Ligno & Lapide. *Coelator* & *Scalptor* insculpit *Figuras,* 10. & *Characteres, Coelo,* 9. Ligno, Aeri. aliisque Metallis.

Looking-glasses. - LXXX. - Specularia.

Looking-glasses, 1. are provided that Men may see themselves.

Spectacles, 2. that he may see better, who hath a weak sight.

Things afar off are seen in a *Perspective Glass,* 3. as things near at hand.

A *Flea* appeareth in a *muliplying-glass,* 4. like a little hog. The Rays of the Sun, burn wood through a *Burning-glass,* 5.

Specularia, parantur, ut homines intueantur seipsos.

Perspicilla, 2. ut cernat acius qui habet visum debilem.

Remota videntur per *telescopium,* 3. ut proxima. *Pulex,* 4. in *Microscopio* apparet ut porcellus. Radii Solis accendunt ligna per *Vitrum urens,* 5,

The Cooper. - LXXXI. - Vietor.

The *Cooper,* 1. having an *Apron,* 2, tied about him, maketh *Hoops* of *Hazel-rods,* 3. upon a *cutting-block,* 4. with a *Spoke-Shave,* 5. and *Lags,* 6. of *Timber.*

Of *Lags* he maketh *Hogsheads,* 7. and *Pipes,* 8. with two *Heads;* and *Tubs,* 9. *Soes,* 10. *Flaskets,* 11. *Buckets,* 12. with one Bottom. Then he bindeth them with *Hoops,* 13. which he tyeth fast with small *Twigs,* 15. by means of a *Cramp-iron,* 14. and he fitteth them on with a *Mallet,* 16. and a *Driver,* 17.

Vietor, 1. amictus *Praecinctorio,* 2. facit *Circulos,* è *Virgis Colurnis,* 3, super *Sellam incisoriam,* 4. *Scalpro bimanubriato,* 5. & *Assulas,* 6. ex *Ligno.*

Ex Assulis conficit *Dolia,* 7. & *Cupas,* 8. *Fundo* bino; turn *Lacus,* 9. *Labra,* 10. *Pitynas* [Trimodia], 11. & *Situlas,* 12. fundo uno.

Postea vincit *Circulis,* 13. quos ligat *Viminibus,* 15. ope *Falcis vietorice,* 14. & aptat *Tudite,* 16. ac *Tudicula,* 17.

The Roper, and the Cordwainer. - LXXXII. - Restio, & Lorarius.

The *Roper,* 1. twisteth *Cords,* 2. of *Tow,* or *Hemp,* 4. (which he wrappeth about himself) by the turning of a *Wheel,* 3.

Thus are made first *Cords,* 5. then *Ropes,* 6, and at last, *Cables,* 7.

The *Cord-wainer,* 8. cutteth great *Thongs,* 10. *Bridles,* 11. *Girdles,* 12. *Sword-belts,* 13. *Pouches,* 14. *Port-mantles,* 15. &c. out of a *Beast-hide,* 9.

Restio, 1. contorquet *Funes,* 2. è *Stupa,* 4. vel *Cannabi,* quam circumdat sibi agitatione *Rotulae,* 3.

Sic fiunt, primò *Funiculi,* 5. tum *Restes,* 6. tandem *Rudentes,* 7.

Lorarius, 8, scindit *Loramenta,* 10. *Froena,* 11. *Cingula,* 12. *Baltheos,* 13. *Crumenas,* 14. *Hippoperas,* 15, &c. de *corio bubulo,* 9.

The Traveller. - LXXXIII. - Viator.

A *Traveller,* 1. beareth on his shoulders on a *Budget,* 2. those things which his *Satchel,* 3. or *Pouch,* 4. cannot hold. He is covered with a *Cloak,* 5.

He holdeth a *Staff,* 6. in his hand wherewith to bear up himself.

He hath need of *Provision for the way,* as also of a pleasant and merry *Companion,* 7.

Let him not forsake the *High-road,* 9. for a *Footway,* 8. unless it be a *beaten Path.*

By-ways, 10. and *places where two ways meet,* 11. deceive and lead men aside into *uneven-places,* 12. so do not *By-paths,* 13. and *Cross-ways,* 14.

Let him therefore enquire of *those he meeteth,* 15. which way he must go; and let him take heed of *Robbers,* 16. as in the *way,* so also in the *Inn,* 17. where he lodgeth all Night.

Viator, 1. portat humeris in *Bulga,* 2. quae non capit *Funda,* 3. vel *Marsupium,* 4. Tegitur *Lacernâ,* 5.

Tenet *Baculum,* 6. Manu quo se fulciat. Opus habet *Viatico,* ut & fido & facundo *Comite,* 7.

Non deserat *Viam regiam* propter *Semitam,* 8, nisi sit *Callis tritus.*

Avia, 10. & *Bivia,* 11. fallunt & seducunt, in *Salebras,* 12. non aequè *Tramites,* 13. & *Compita,* 14.

Sciscitet igitur *obvios,* 15. quà sit eundum; & caveat *Praedones,* 16. ut in viâ, sic etiam in *Diversorio,* 17. ubi pernoctat.

The Horse-man - LXXXIV. – Eques.

The *Horse-man,* 1. setteth a *Saddle,* 2. on his *Horse,* 3. and girdeth it on with a *Girth,* 4.

He layeth a *Saddle-cloth,* 5. also upon him.

He decketh him with *Trappings,* a *Fore-stall,* 6, a *Breast-cloth,* 7. and a *Crupper,* 8.

Then he getteth upon his Horse, putteth his feet into the *Stirrops,* 9. Taketh the *Bridle-rein,* 10. 11, in his left hand, wherewith he guideth and holdeth the Horse.

Then he putteth to his *Spurs,* 12. and setteth him on with a *Switch,* 13. and holdeth him in with a *Musrol,* 14. The *Holsters,* 15, hang down from the *Pummel* of the *Saddle,* 16. in which the *Pistols,* 17. are put.

The Rider is clad in a short *Coat,* 18. his *Cloak* being tyed behind him, 19.

A *Post,* 20. is carried on Horseback at full Gallop.

Eques, 1. imponit *Equo,* 2. *Ephippium,* 3. idque succingit *Cingulo,* 4.

Insternit etiam *Dorsuale,* 5 Ornat eum *Phaleris, Frontali,* 6. *Antilena,* 7. & *Postilena,* 8.

Deinde insilit in Equum, indit pedes *Stapedibus,* 9. capessit *Lorum* (habenam), 10. *Freni,* 11. sinistrâ quo flectit, & retinet Equum.

Tum admovet *Calcaria,* 12. incitatque *Virgula,* 13. & coërcet *Postomide,* 14. *Bulgae,* 15. pendent ex *Apice Ephippii,* 16. quibus *Sclopi,* 17. inseruntur.

Ipse Eques induitur *Chlamyde,* 18. *Lacernâ* revinctâ, 19. à tergo.

Veredarius, 20. fertur Equo cursim.

Carriages. - LXXXV - Vehicula.

We are carried on a *Sled,* 1. over Snow and Ice.

A Carriage with one Wheel, is called a *Wheelbarrow,* 2. with two Wheels, a *Cart,* 3. with four Wheels, a *Wagon,* which is either a *Timber-wagon,* 4. or a *Load-wagon,* 5.

The parts of the Wagon are, the *Neep* (or draught-tree), 6. the *Beam,* 7. the *Bottom,* 8. and the *Sides,* 9.

Then the *Axle-trees,* 10. about which the *Wheels* run, the *Lin-pins,* 11. and *Axletree-staves,* 12. being fastened before them.

The *Nave,* 13. is the groundfast of the *Wheel,* 14. from which come twelve *Spokes,* 15.

The *Ring* encompasseth these, which is made of six *Felloes,* 16. and as many *Strakes,* 17. *Hampiers* and *Hurdles,* 18, are set in a Wagon.

Vehimur *Trahâ,* 1. super Nivibus & Glacie.

Vehiculum unirotum, dicitur *Pabo,* 2. birotum, *Carrus,* 3. quadrirotum, *Currus,* qui vel *Sarracum,* 4. vel *Plaustrum,* 5. Partes Currûs sunt, *Temo,* 6. *Jugum,* 7. *Compages,* 8. *Spondae,* 9.

Tum *Axes,* 10. circa quos *Rotae* currunt, *Paxillis,* 11. & *Obicibus,* 12. praefixis.

Modiolus, 13. est Basis *Rotae,* 14. ex quo prodeunt duodecim *Radii,* 15.

Orbile ambit hos, compositum, è sex *Absidibus,* 16. & totidem *Canthis,* 17. *Corbes* & *Crates,* 18. imponuntur Currui.

Carrying to and fro. - LXXXVI. - Vectura.

The *Coach-man,* 1. joineth a *Horse fit to match a Saddle-horse,* 2, 3. to the *Coach-tree,* with *Thongs* or *Chains,* 5. hanging down from the *Collar,* 4.

Then he sitteth upon the *Saddle-horse,* and driveth them that go before him, 6. with a *Whip,* 7. and guideth them with a *String,* 8

He greaseth the *Axle-tree* with *Axle-tree grease* out of a *Grease-pot,* 9. and stoppeth the wheel with a *Trigen,* 10. in a steep descent.

And thus the Coach is driven along the *Wheel-ruts,* 11.

Great Persons are carryed *with six Horses,* 12. by two *Coachmen,* in a Hanging-wagon, which is called a *Coach,* 13 .

Others *with two Horses,* 14. in a *Chariot,* 15.

Horse Liiters, 16, 17. are carried by two Horses.

They use *Pack-Horses,* instead of *Waggons,* thorow *Hills* that are not passable, 18.

Auriga, 1. jungit *Parippum,* 2. *Sellario,* 3. ad *Temonem, Loris* vel *Catenis,* 5. dependentibus de *Helcio,* 4. Deinde insidet *Sellario,* agit ante se antecessores, 6. *Scuticâ,* 7. & flectit *Funibus,* 8. Ungit *Axem Axungiâ,* ex *vase unguentorio,* 9. & inhibet rotam Sufflamine, 10. in praecipiti descensu.

Et sic aurigatur per *Orbitas,* 11.

Magnates vehuntur *Sejugibus,* 12. duobus *Rhedariis,* Curru pensili, qui vocatur *Carpentum* (Pilentum), 13.

Alii *Bijugibus,* 14. *Essedo,* 15.

Arcerae, 16. , *Lacticae,* 17. portantur à duobus Equis.

Utuntur *Jumentis Clitellariis,* loco *Curruum,* per *montes* invios, 18.

Passing over Waters. - LXXXVII. - Transitus Aquarum.

Lest he that is to pass over a River should be wet,

Bridges, 1. were invented for Carriages, and *Foot-bridges,* 2. for Foot-men.

If a river have a *Foord,* 3. it *is waded over,* 4.

Flotes, 5. also are made of Timber pinned together; or *Ferry-boats,* 6. of planks laid close together for fear they should rcceive Water.

Besides *Scullers,* 7. are made, which are rowed with an *Oar,* 8. or *Pole,* 9. or haled with an *Haling-rope,* 10.

Trajecturus tlumen ne madefiat, *Pontes,* 1. excogitati sunt pro Vehiculis & *Ponticuli,* 2. pro Peditibus.

Si Flumen habet *Vadum,* 3. *vadatur,* 4.

Rates, etiam struuntur ex compactis tignis; vel *Pontones,* 6. ex trabibus consolidatis, ne excipiant aquam.

Porrò *Lintres* (Lembi), 7. fabricantur, qui aguntur *Remo,* 8. vel *Conto,* 9. aut trahuntur *Remulco,* 10.

Swimming. - LXXXVIII. - Natatus.

Men are wont also to swim over Waters upon a *bundle of flags,* 1. and besides upon blown *Beast-bladders,* 2. and after, by throwing their *Hands* and *Feet,* 3. abroad.

And at last they learned *to tread the water,* 4. being plunged up to the girdle-stead, and carrying their Cloaths upon their head.

A *Diver,* 5. can swim also under the water like a Fish.

Solent etiam tranare aquas super *scirpeum fascem,* 1. porrò super inflatas *boum Vesicas,* 2. deinde liberè jactatu *Manuum Pedumque,* 3.

Tandem didicerunt *calcare aquam,* 4. immersi cingulo tenus & gestantes Vestes supra caput.

Urinator, 5. etiam natare potest sub aquâ, ut Piscis.

A Galley. - LXXXIX. - Navis actuaria.

A *Ship* furnished with *Oars,* 1. is a *Barge,* 2. or a *Foyst,* &c. in which the *Rowers,* 3. sitting on *Seats,* 4. by the *Oar-rings,* row, by striking the water with the *Oars,* 5.

The Ship-master, 6. standing in the Fore-castle, and the Steers-man, 7. sitting at the Stern, and holding the Rudder, 8. steer the Vessel.

Navis instructa *Remis,* 1 . est *Uniremis,* 2. vel *Biremis,* &c. in quâ *Remiges,* 3. considentes pre *Transtra,* 4. ad *Scalmos,* remigant pellendo aquam *Remis.*

Proreta, 6. stans in *Prora,* & *Gubernator,* 7. sedens in *Puppi,* tenensque *Clavum,* 8. gubernant *Navigium.*

A Merchant-ship. - XC. - Navis oneraria.

A *Ship,* 1. is driven onward not by Oars, but by the only force of the Winds.

In it is a *Mast,* 2. set up, fastened with *Shrowds,* 3. on all sides to the *main-chains,* to which the *Sail-yards,* 4. are tied, and the *Sails,* 5. to these, which are *spread open,* 6. to the wind, and are hoysed by *Bowlings,* 7.

The Sails are the *Main-sail,* 8. the *Trinket,* or *Fore-sail,* 9. the *Misen-sail* or *Poop-sail,* 10.

The *Beak,* 11. is in the *Fore-deck.*

The *Ancient,* 12. is placed in the *Stern.*

On the Mast is the *Foretop,* 13. the *Watch-tower* of the Ship, and over the *Fore-top* a *Vane,* 14. to shew which way the Wind standeth.

The ship is stayed with an *Anchor,* 15. The depth is fathomed with a *Plummet,* 16. Passengers walk up and down the *Decks,* 17. The Sea men run to and fro through the *Hatches,* And thus, even Seas are passed over.

Navigium, 1. impellitur, non remis, sed solâ vi Ventorum.

In illo *Malus,* 2. erigitur, firmatus *Funibus,* 3. undique ad *Oras Navis,* cui annectuntur *Antennae,* 4. His, *Vela,* 5. quae *expanduntur,* 6. ad Ventum & *Versoriis,* 7. versantur.

Vela sunt *Artemon,* 8. *Dolon,* 9. & *Epidromus,* 10. *Rostrum,* 11. est in *Prora. Signum* (vexillum), 12. ponitur in *Puppi.*

In Malo est *Cordis,* 13. *Specula* Navis & supra *Galeam Aplustre,* 14. Ventorum Index.

Navis sistitur *Anchorâ,* 15. Profunditas exploratur *Bolide,* 16. Navigantes deambulant in *Tabulato,* 17. Nautae cursitant per *Foros,* 18. Atque ita, etiam Maria trajiciuntur.

Ship-wreck. – XCI. - Naufragium.

When a *Storm,* 1. ariseth on a sudden, they strike *Sail,* 2. lest the Ship should be dashed against *Rocks,* 3 or light upon *Shelves,* 4.

If they cannot hinder her they suffer *Ship-Wreck,* 5.

And then the men, the *Wares,* and all things are miserably lost.

Nor doth the *Sheat-anchor,* 6. being cast with a *Cable,* do any good.

Some escape, either on a *Plank,* 7. and by swimming, or in the *Boat,* 8.

Part of the Wares, with the dead folks, is carried out of the *Sea,* 9. upon the Shoars.

Cum *Procella,* 1. oritur repentè contrahunt *Vela,* 2. ne Navis ad *Scopulos,* 3. allidatur, aut incidat in *Brevia* (Syrtes), 4.

Si non possunt prohibere patiuntur *Naufragium,* 5.

Tum Homines, *Merces,* omnia miserabiliter pereunt.

Neque hic *Sacra anchora,* 6. *Rudenti* jacta quidquam adjuvat.

Quidam evadunt, vel *tabula,* 7. ac enatando, vel *Scapha,* 8.

Pars Mercium cum mortuis a *Mari,* 9. in littora defertur.

Writing. – XCII. - Ars Scriptoria.

The Ancients writ in *Tables done over with wax* with a brazen *Poitrel,* 1. with the *sharp end,* 2. whereof letters were engraven and rubbed out again with the *broad end,* 3.

Afterwards they writ *Letters* with a *small Reed,* 4.

We use a *Goose-quill,* 5. the *Stem,* 6. of which we make with a *Pen-knife,* 7. then we dip the *Neb* in an *Ink-horn,* 8. which is stopped with a *Stopple,* 9. and we put our *Pens,* into a *Pennar,* 10.

We dry a Writing with *Blotting-paper,* or *Calis-sand* out of a *Sand-box,* 11.

And we indeed write from the left hand towards the right, 12. the *Hebrews* from the right hand towards the left, 13. the *Chinese* and other *Indians,* from the top downwards, 14.

Veteres scribebant in *Tabellis ceratis* aeneo *Stilo,* 1. cujus *parte cuspidata,* 2. exarabantur literae, rursum vero obliteraban tur *planâ.*

Deinde *Literas* pingebant *subtili Calamo,* 4. Nos utimur, *Anserina Penna,* 5. cujus *Caulem,* 6. temperamus *Scalpello,* 7. tum intingimus *Crenam* in *Atramentario,* 8. quod obstruitur *Operculo,* 9. & Pennas recondimus in *Calamario,* 10.

Siccamus Scripturam *Chartâ blbulâ,* vel *Arenâ scriptoria,* ex *Theca Pulveraria,* Et nos quidem scribimus â sinistra dextrorsum, 12. *Hebraei* â dextrâ sinistrorsum, 13. *Chinenses* & *Indi* alii, â summo deorsum, 14.

Paper. - XCIII. - Papyrus.

The Ancients used *Beech-Boards,* 1. or *Leaves,* 2. as also *Barks,* 3. of *Trees,* especially of an Egyptian Shrub, which was called *Papyrus.*

Now *Paper* is in use which the *Paper-maker* maketh in a *Paper-mill,* 4. of *Linen rags,* 5. stamped to *Mash,* 6. which being taken up in *Frames,* 7. he spreadeth into *Sheets,* 8. and setteth them in the Air that they may be dryed.

Twenty-five of these make a *Quire,* 9. twenty Quires a *Ream,* 10. and ten of these a *Bale of Paper,* 11.

That which is to last long is written on *Parchment,* 12.

Veteres utebantur *Tabulis Faginis,* 1. aut *Foliis,* 2. ut & *Libris,* 3. *Arborum;* praesertim Arbusculae Aegyptiae, cui nomen erat Papyrus.

Nunc *Charta* est in usu, quam *Chattopoeus* in *mola Papyracea,* 4. conficit è *Linteis vetustis,* 5. in *Pulmentum* contusis, 6. quod haustum *Normulis,* 7. diducit in *Plagulas,* 8. exponitque aëri, ut siccentur.

Harum XXV. faciunt *Scapum,* 9. XX. Scapi *Volumen minus,* 10. horum X. *Volumen majus,* 11.

Duraturum diu scribitur in *Membrana,* 12.

Printing. - XCIV. - Typographia.

The *Printer* hath *metal Letters* in a large number put into *Boxes,* 5. The *Compositor,* 1. taketh them out one by one and according to the *Copy,* (which he hath fastened before him in a *Visorum,* 2.) composeth words in a *Composing-stick,* 3. till a *Line* be made; he putteth these in a *Gally,* 4. till a *Page,* 6. be made, and these again in a *Form,* 7. and he locketh them up in *Iron Chases,* 8. with *Coyns,* 9. lest they should drop out, and putteth them under the *Press,* 10.

Then the *Press-man* beateth it over with *Printers Ink,* by means of *Balls,* 11. spreadeth upon it the Papers put in the *Frisket,* 12. which being put under the *Spindle,* 14. on the *Coffin,* 13. and pressed down with a *Bar,* 15. he maketh to take impression.

Typographus habet *Typos* Metallos, magno numero distributos per *Loculamenta,* 5.

Typotheta, 1. eximit illos singulatim, & secundum *exemplar,* (quod habet praefixum sibi *Retinaculo,* 2.) componit Verba *Gnomone,* 3. donec versus fiat; hos indit *Formae,* 4. donee *Pagina,* 6. fiat; has iterum *Tabulâ compositoriâ,* 7. coarctaque eos *Marginibus ferreis,* 8. ope *Cochlearum,* 9. ne dilabantur, ac subjicit *Prelo,* 10.

Tum *Impressor* illinit.

Atramento impressorio ope *Pilarum,* 11. super imponit Chartas inditas *Operculo,* 12. quas subditas *Trochleae,* 14. in *Tigello,* 13. & impressas *Suculâ,* 15. facit imbibere typos.

The Booksellers Shop. – XCV. - Bibliopolium.

The *Bookseller,* 1. selleth *Books* in a *Booksellers Shop,* 2. of which he writeth a *Catalogue,* 3. The Books are placed on *Shelves,* 4. and are laid open for use upon a *Desk,* 5. A Multitude of Books is called a *Library,* 6.

Bibliopola, 1. vendit *Libros* in *Bibliopolio,* 2. quorum conscribit *Catalogum,* 3. Libri disponuntur per *Repositoria,* 4. & exponuntur ad usum, super *Pluteum,* 5. Multitudo Librorum vocatur *Bibliotheca,* 6.

The Book-binder. – XCVI. - Bibliopegus.

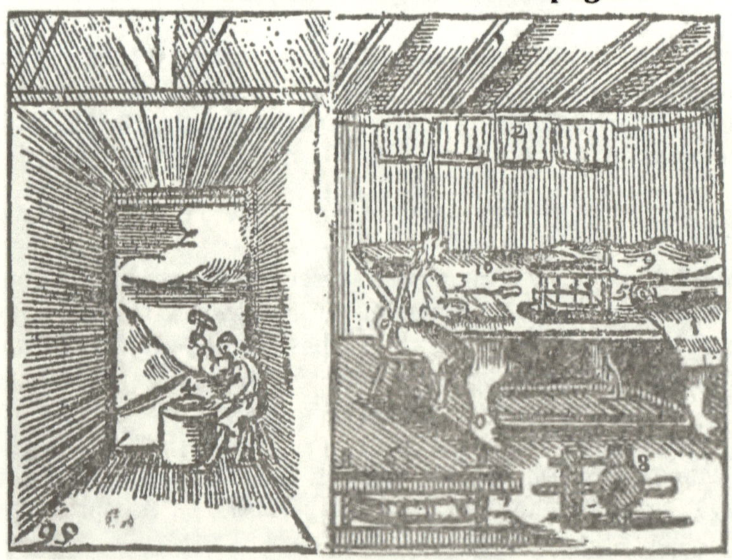

In times past they glewed Paper to Paper, .and rolled them up together into one *Roll,* 1.

At this day the *Book-binder* bindeth Books, whilst he wipeth, 2. over Papers steept in *Gum-water,* and then foldeth them together, 3. beatheth with a hammer, 4. then stitcheth them up, 5. presseth them in a *Press,* 6. which hath two *Screws,* 7. glueth them on the back, cutteth off the edges with a *round Knife,* 8. and at last covereth them with *Parchment* or *Leather,* 9. maketh them handsome, and setteth on *Clasps,* 10.

Olim agglutinabant Chartam Chartae, convolvebantque eas in unum *Volumen,* 1.

Hodiè *Compactor* compingit Libros, dum tergit, 2. chartas maceratas *aquâ glutinosâ,* deinde complicat, 3. malleat, 4. tum consuit, 5. conprimit *Prelo,* 6. quod habet duos *Cochleas,* 7. conglutinat dorso, demarginat rotundo *Cultro,* 8. tandem vestit *Membranâ* vel *Corio,* 9. efformat, & affigit *Uncinulos,* 10.

A Book. - XCVII. - Liber.

A *Book* as to its outward shape, is either in *Folio,* 1. or in *Quarto,* 2. in *Octavo,* 3. in *Duodecimo,* 4. either *made to open Side-wise,* 5. or *Long-wise,* 6. with *Brazen Clasps,* 7. or *Strings,* 8. and *Square-bofles,* 9.

Within are *Leaves,* 10. with two *Pages,* sometimes divided with *Columns,* 11. and *Marginal Notes,* 12.

Liber, quoad exteriorem formant est vel in *Folia,* 1. vel in *Quarto,* 2. in *Octavo,* 3. in *Duodecimo,* 4. vel *Columnatus,* 5. vel *Linguatus,* 6. cum *Aeneis Clausuris,* 7. vel *Ligulis,* 8. & *angularibus Bullis,* 9.

Intùs sunt *Folia,* 10. duabis *Paginis,* aliquando *Columnis,* 11. divisa cumq; *Notis Marginalibus,* 12.

A School. - XCVII. - Schola.

A *School,* 1. is a Shop in which *Young Wits* are fashion'd to vertue, and it is distinguish'd into *Forms.*

The *Master,* 2. sitteth in a *Chair,* 3. the *Scholars,* 4. in *Forms,* 5. he teacheth, they learn.

Some things are writ down before them with *Chalk* on a *Table,* 6.

Some sit at a Table, and write, 7. he mendeth their Faults, 8.

Some stand and rehearse things committed to memory, 9.

Some talk together, 10. and behave themselves wantonly and carelessly; these are chastised with a *Ferrula.* 11. and a *Rod.* 12.

Schola, 1. est Officina, in quâ *Novelli Animi* formantur ad virtutem, & distinguitur in *Classes.*

Praeceptor, 2. sedet in *Cathedra,* 3. *Discipuli,* 4. in *Subselliis,* 5. ille docet, hi discunt.

Quaedam praescribuntur illis *Cretâ* in *Tabella,* 6.

Quidam sedent ad Mensam, & scribunt, 7. ipse corrigit Mendas, 8.

Quidam stant, & recitant mandata memoriae, 9.

Quidam confabulantur, 10. ac gerunt se petulantes, & negligentes; hi castigantur *Ferulâ* (baculo), 11. & *Virgâ,* 12.

The Study. - XCIX. - Museum.

The *Study,* 1. is a place where a Student, 2, apart from Men, sitteth alone, addicted to his *Studies,* whilst he readeth *Books,* 3. which being within his reach he layeth open upon a *Desk,* 4. and picketh all the best things out of them into his own *Manual,* 5. or marketh them in them with a *Dash,* 6. or a *little Star,* 7. in the *Margent.*

Being to sit up late. he setteth a *Candle,* 8. on a *Candlestick,* 9. which is snuffed with *Snuffers,* 10. before the Candle he placeth a *Screen,* 11. which is green, that it may not hurt his eye-sight; richer Persons use a *Taper,* for a Tallow-candle stinketh and smoaketh.

A *Letter,* 12. is wrapped up, writ upon, 13. and sealed, 14. Going abroad by night, he maketh use of a *Lanthorn,* 15. or a *Torch,* 16.

Museum, 1. est locus ubi Studiosus, 2. secretus ab Hominibus, sedet solus deditus *Studiis,* dum lectitat *Libros,* 3. quos penes se & exponit super *Pluteum,* 4. & excerpit optima quaeque ex illis in *Manuale* suum, 5. notat in illis *Liturâ,* 6. vel *Asterisco,* 7. ad *Margiem.*

Lucubraturus, elevat *Lychnum* (*Canelam*), 8. in *Candelabra,* 9. qui emungitur *Emunctorio,* 10. ante Lynchum collocat *Umbraculum,* 11. quod viride est, ne hebetet oculorum aciem; opulentiores utuntur *Cereo* nam *Candela sebacea* foetet & fugimat.

Epistola, 12. complicatur, inscribitur, 13. & obsignatur, 14. Prodiens noctu utitur *Lanterna,* 15. vel *Face,* 16.

Arts belonging to Speech. - C. - Artes Sermones.

Grammar, 1. is conversant about *Letters,* 2. of which it maketh *Words,* 3. and teacheth how to utter, write, 4. put together and part them rightly.

Rhetorick, 5. doth as it were paint, 6. a rude form, 7. of Speech with *Oratory Flourishes,* 8. such as are *Figures, Elegancies, Adagies, Apothegms, Sentences, Similies, Hierogylphicks,* &c.

Poetry, 9. gathereth these *Flowers of Speech,* 10. and tieth them as it were into a little *Garland,* 11. and so making of *Prose* a *Poem,* it maketh several sorts of Verses and Odes, and is therefore crowned with a Laurel, 12.

Musick, 13. setteth *Tunes,* 14. with *pricks,* to which it setteth words, and so singeth alone, or in *Consort,* or by Voice, or Musical Instruments, 15.

Grammatica. 1. versatur circa *Literas,* 2. ex quibus componit *Voces, verba,* 3. docetque eloqui, scribere, 4. construere, distinguere (interpungere) eas recte.

Rhetorica, 5. pingit, 6. quasi rudem *formam,* 7. Sermon is *Oratoriis Pigmentis,* 8. ut sunt *Figurae, Elegantiae, Adagia* (proverbia) *Apothegmata, Sententiae* (Gnomae) *Similia, Hieroglyphica,* &c. *Poesis,* 9. coliigit hos *Flores Orationis,* 10. & colligat quasi in *Corallam,* 11. atque ita, faciens è *prosa ligatam orationem,* componi varia *Carmina* & *Hymnos* (*Odas*) ac propterea coronatur *Lauru,* 12.

Musica, 13. componit *Melodias,* 14. *Notis,* quibus aptat verba, atque ita cantat sola vel *Concentu* (*Symphonia*), aut voce aut Instrumentis Musicis, 15.

Musical Instruments. - CI. - Instrumenta musica.

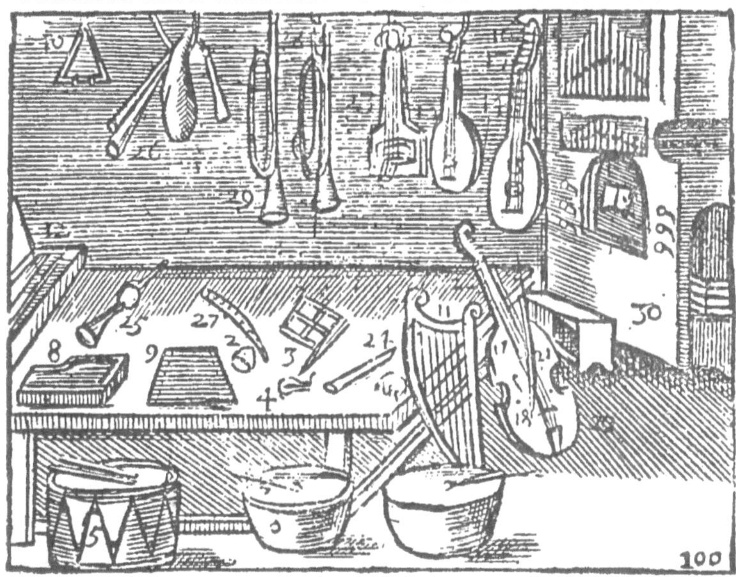

Musical Instruments are those which make a sound:

First, when they are beaten upon, as a *Cymbal,* 1. with a *Pestil,* a *little Bell,* 2. with an *Iron pellet* within; or *Rattle,* 3. by tossing it about: a *Jews-Trump,* 4. being put to the mouth, with the fingers; a *Drum,* 5 . and a *Kettle,* 6. with a *Drum-stick,* 7. as also the *Dulcimer,* 8. with thc *Shcphcrds-harp,* 9. and the *Tymbrel,* 10.

Secondly, upon which *strings* are stretched, and struck upon, as the *Psaltery,* 11. and the *Virginals,* 12. with both hands; the *Lute,* 13. in which is the *Neck,* 14. the *Belly,* 15, the *Pegs,* 16. by which the *Strings,* 17. are stretched upon the *Bridge,* 18.) the *Cittern,* 19. with the right hand only, the *Vial,* 20. with a *Bow,* 21, and the *Harp,* 23. with a Wheel within, which is turned about: the *Stops,* 22. in every one are touched with the left hand.

At last, those which are blown, as with the mouth, the *Flute,* 24. the *Shawm,* 25. the *Bag-pipe,* 26. the *Cornet,* 27. the *Trumpet,* 28, 29, or with *Bellows,* as a *pair of Organs,* 30.

Musica instrumenta sunt quae edunt vocem:

Primò, cum pulsantur, ut *Cymbalum,* 1. *Pistillo, Tintinnabulum,* 2. intus *Globulo ferreo, Crepitaculum,* 3. circumversando; *Crembalum,* 4. ori admotum, Digito; *Tympanum,* 5. & *Ahenum,* 6. *Claviculâ,* 7. ut & *Sambuca,* 8. cum *Organo pastoritio,* 9. & *Sistrum* (Crotalum), 10. Secundò, in quibus *Chordae* intenduntur & plectuntur ut *Nablium,* 11. cum *Clavircordio,* 12. utrâque manu; *Testudo* (Chelys), 13. (in quâ *Jugum,* 14. *Magadium,* 15. & *Verticilli,* 16. quibus *Nervi,* 17. intenduntur super *Ponticulam,* 18.) & *Cythara,* 19, Dexterâ tantum, *Pandura,* 20. *Plectro,* 21. & *Lyra,* 23. intus rotâ, quae versatur: Dimensiones, 22. in singulis tanguntur sinistra.

Tandem quae inflantur, ut Ore, *Fistula* (Tibia), 24. *Gingras,* 25. *Tibia utricularis,* 26. *Lituus,* 27. *Tuba,* 28. *Buccina,* 29. vel *Follibus,* ut *Organum pneumaticum,* 30.

Philosophy. - CII. - Philosophia.

The *Naturalist,* 1. vieweth all the works of God in the World.

The Supernaturalist, 2. searches out the Causes and Effects of things.

The Arithmetician, reckoneth numbers, by adding, subtracting, multiplying and dividing; and that either by Cyphers, 3. on a Slate, or by Counters, 4. upon a Desk.

Country people reckon, 5. with figures of tens, X. 2iTvdi figures of five , V. by twelves, fifteens, and threescores.

Physicus, 1. speculatur omnia Dei Opera in Mundo,

Metaphysicus, 2. perscrutatur *Causas,* & rerum *Effecta.*

Arithmeticus computat *numeros,* addendo, subtrahendo, multiplicando, dividendo; idque vel *Cyphris,* 3. in *Palimocesto,* vel *Calculis,* 4. super *Abacum.*

Rustici numerant, 5, *Decussibus,* X. & *Quincuncibus,* V. per *Duodenas, Quindenas,* & *Sexagenas.*

Geometry. - CIII. - Geometria.

A *Geometrician* measureth the *height* of a *Tower,* 1...2. or the *distance* of *places,* 3 ... 4. either with a *Quadrant,* 5. or a *Jacob's-staff,* 6.

He maketh out the *Figures of things,* with *Lines,* 7. *Angles,* 8. and *Circles,* 9. by a *Rule,* 10. a *Square,* 11. and a *pair of Compasses,* 12. Out of these arise an *Oval,* 13. a *Triangle,* 14. a *Quadrangle,* 15. and other figures.

Geometra metitur *Altitudinem Turris,* 1... 2. aut *dlstantium Locorum,* 3 ...4. sive *Quadrante,* 5. sive *Radio,* 6.

Designat *Figuras rerum Lineis,* 7, Angulis, 8. & *Circulis,* 9. ad *Regulam,* 10. *Normam.* 1 1. & *Circinum,* 12. Ex his oriuntur *Cylindrus,* 13. *Trigonus* 14. *Tetragonus,* 15. & aliae figurae.

The Celestial Sphere. - CIV. - Sphera caelestis.

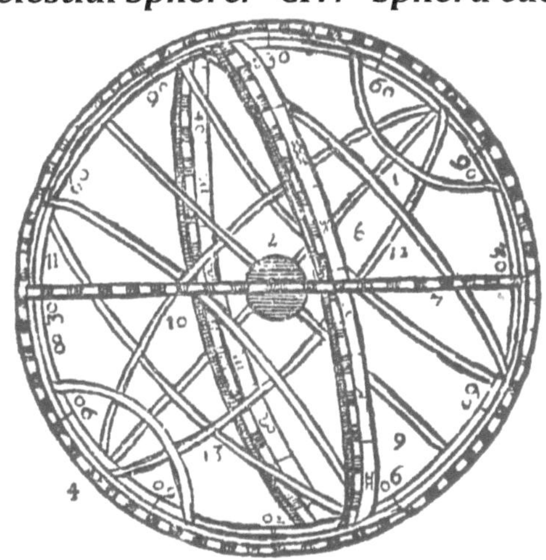

Astronomy considereth the *motion of the Stars, Astrology* the Effects of them.

The *Globe of Heaven* is turned about upon an *Axle-tree,* 1. about the Globe of the *Earth,* 2. in the space of XXIV. hours.

The *Pole-stars,* or *Pole,* the *Arctick,* 3. the *Antarctick,* 4. conclude the *Axle-tree* at both ends.

The *Heaven* is full of Stars every where.

There are reckoned above a *thousand fixed Stars;* but of *Constellations towards the North,* XXI. *towards the South,* XVI.

Add to these the XII, *signs* of the *Zodiaque,* 5. every one XXX. degrees, whose names are *Aries, Taurus, Gemini, Cancer, Leo, Virgo, Libra, Scorpius, Sagittarius, Capricor, Aquarius, Pisces.*

Under this move the seven *Wandring-stars* which they call *Planets,* whose way is a circle in the middle of the Zodiack, called the *Ecliptick,* 6.

Other Circles are the *Horizon,* 7. the *Meridian,* 8. the *Equator,* 9. the two *Colures,* the one of the *Equinocts,* 10. (of the *Spring* when the sun entreth into Aries; *Autumnal* when it entreth in Libra) the other of the *Solstices,* 11. (of the *Summer,* when the Sun entreth into Cancer of the *Winter* when it entreth into Capricor) the *Tropicks,* the *Tropick of Cancer,* 12. the *Tropick of Capricorn,* 13. and the two *Polar Circles,* 14...15.

Astronomia considerat *motus Astrorum, Astrologia* eorum Effectus.

Globus Coeli volvitur super *Axem,* 1. circa *globum terrae,* 2. spacio XXIV. horarum.

Stellae polares, Arcticus, 3. *Antarcticus,* 4. finiunt *Axem* utrinque.

Caelum est Stellatum undique.

Stellarum fixarum numerantur plus *mille; Siderum* verò *Septentrionarium,* XXI. *Meridionalium,* XVI.

Adde *Signa,* XII. *Zodiaci,* 5. quodlibet graduum, XXX. quorum nomina sunt *Aries, Taurus, Gem. Cancer, Leo, Virgo, Libra, Scorpius, Sagittarius, Capricorn, Aquarius, Pisces.*

Sub hoc cursitant *Stellae errantes* VII. quas vocant *Planetas,* quorum via est Circulvs, in medio Zodiaci, dictus *Ecliptica,* 6.

Alii Circuli sunt *Horizon,* 7. *Meridianus,* 8. *Equator,* 9. duo *Coluri,* alter *Aequinoxiorum,* 10. (*Verni,* quando sol ingreditur Aries; *Autumnalis,* quando ingreditur Libra) alter *Solsticiorum,* 11. (Aestivi, quando sol ingreditur Cancer, *Hyberni,* quando sol ingreditur Capricorn) duo *Tropici, Tr. Cancri,* 12. Tr. *Capricorni,* 13. & duo *Polares,* 14. ... 15.

The Aspects of the Planets. - CIV. - Planetarum Aspectus.

The *Moon* runneth through the *Zodiack* every *Month.*

The *Sun,* in a Year. *Mercury,* and *Venus* about the Sun, the one in a hundred and fifteen, the other in 585 days. *Mars,* in two years; *Jupiter,* in almost twelve; *Saturn,* in thirty years.

Hereupon they meet variously among themselves, and have mutual Aspects one towards another. As here the sun and Mercury, are in *Conjunction,* sun and *Moon* in *Opposition,* sun and Saturn, in a *Trine Aspect, sun* and Jupiter in a *Quartile,* sun and Mars in a *Sextile.*

Luna percurrit *Zodiacum* singulis *Mensibus. Sol,* Anno. *Mercurius* & *Venus,* circa Solem, ilia cxv, haec DLXXXV. Diebus. *Mars,* Biennio; *Jupiter,* ferè duodecim; *Saturnus,* triginta annis. Hinc conveniunt variè inter se & se mutuo adspiciunt. Ut hic sunt, sol Mercurio in *Conjunctione,* sol & Luna in *Opposition,* sol & Saturnus, in *Trigono,*sol & Jupiter in *Quadratura,*sol & Mars in *Sextili.*

The Apparitions of the Moon. - CV. – Phases Lunae.

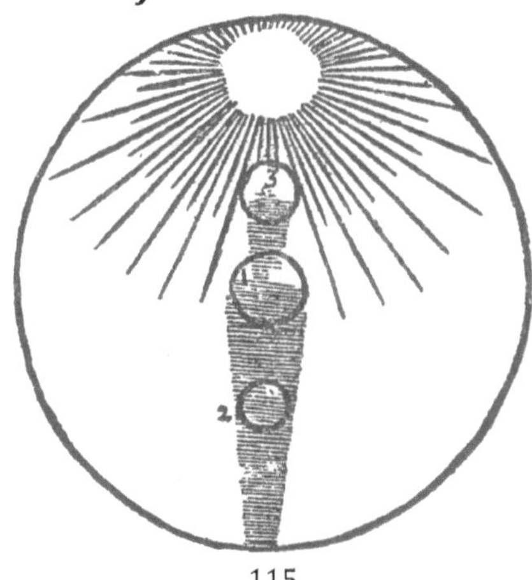

The *Moon* shineth not by her own *Light* but that which is borrowed of the *Sun.*

For the one half of it is always enlightned, the other remaineth darkish. Hereupon we see it in *Conjunction* with the *Sun,* 1. to be obscure, almost none at all; in *Opposition,* 5. whole and clear, (and we call it the *Full Moon;*) sometimes in the half, (and we call it the *Prime,* 3. and *last Quarter,* 7.)

Otherwise it waxeth, 2...4. or waneth, 6...8. and is said to be *horned,* or more than half *round.*

Luna, lucet non sua propria *Luce,* sed mutuatâ a *Sole.*

Nam altera ejus medietas semper illuminatur, altera manet caliginosa.

Hinc videmus, in *Conjunctione Solis,* 1. obscuram, imo nullam: in *Oppositione,* 5. totam & lucidam, (& vocamus *Plenilunium;*) alias dimidiam, (& dicimus *Primam,* 3. & *ultimam Quadram,* 7.) Caeteroqui crescit, 2...4. aut decrescit, 6...8. & vocatur *falcata,* vel *gibbosa.*

The Eclipses. – CVI. - Eclipses.

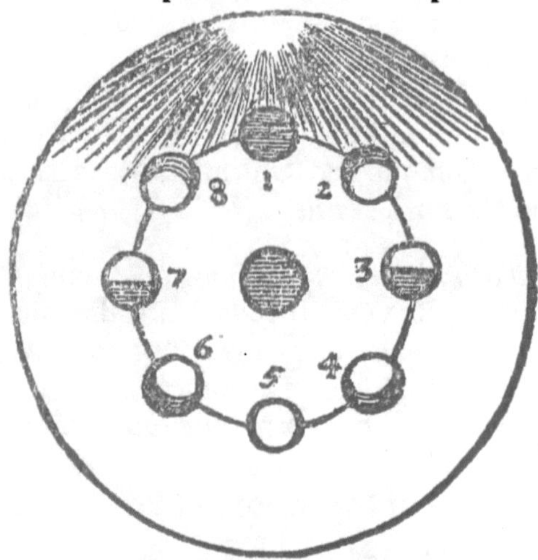

The *Sun* is the fountain of light, inlightning all things, but the *Earth,* 1. and the *Moon,* 2. being shady bodies, are not pierced with its rays, for they cast a shadow upon the place just over against them.

Therefore, when the Moon lighteth into the shadow of the *Earth,* 2. it is darkened, which we call an *Eclipse,* or defect.

But when the *Moon* runneth betwixt the *Sun* and the *Earth,* 3. it covereth it with its shadow; and this we call the *Eclipse* of the *Sun,* because it taketh from us the sight of the *Sun,* and its light; neither doth the *Sun* for all that suffer any thing, but the *Earth.*

Sol est fons Lucis, illuminans omnia; sed *Terra,* 1. & *Luna,* 2. Corpora opaca, non penetrantur ejus radiis, nam jaciunt umbram in locum oppositum.

Ideo cum Luna incidit in umbram *Terrae,* 2. obscuratur quod vocamus *Eclipsin* (deliquium) *Lunae.*

Cum vero *Luna* currit inter *Solem* & *Terram,* 3. obtegit ilium umbrâ suâ; & hoc vocamus *Eclipsin Solis,* quia adimit nobis prospectum *Solis,* & lucem ejus; nec tamen *Sol* patitur aliquid, sed *Terra.*

The terrestial Sphere. - CVII. a - Sphera terrestris.

The *Earth* is round, and therefore to be represented by two *Hemispheres,* a..b.

The Circuit of it is 360 *degrees* (whereof every one maketh 60 *English* Miles or 21600 Miles,) and yet it is but a prick, compared with the World, whereof it is the *Centre.*

They measure Longitude of it by *Climates,* 1. and the *Latitude* by *Parallels,* 2.

The *Ocean,* 3. compasseth it about, and five *Seas* wash it, the *Mediterranean Sea,* 4. the *Baltick Sea,* 5. the *Red Sea,* 6. the *Persian Sea,* 7. and the *Caspian Sea,* 8.

Terra est rotunda, fingenda igitur duobus *Hemispheriis,* a..b,

Ambitus ejus est *graduum* CCCLX. (quorum quisque facit LX. Milliaria *Anglica* vel 21600 Milliarium) & tamen est punctum, collata cum orbe, cujus *Centrum* est.

Longitudinem ejus dimetiuntur *Climatibus,* 1. *Latitudinem,* lineis *Parallelis,* 2.

Oceanus, 3. ambit eam & *Maria* V. perfundunt *Mediterraneum,* 4. *Balticum,* 5. *Erythraeum,* 6. *Persicum,* 7. *Caspium,* 8.

The terrestial Sphere. - CVII. b - Sphera terrestris.

It is divided into V. *Zones,* whereof the II. *frigid ones,* 9...9. are uninhabitable; the II. *Temperate* ones, 10...10. and the *Torrid* one, II. habitable.

Besides it is divided into three *Continents;* this of ours, 12. which is subdivided into *Europe,* 13. *Asia,* 14. *Africa,* 15. *America,* 16. ... 16. (whose Inhabitants are *Antipodes* to us;) and the *South Land,* 17...17. yet unknown.

They that dwell underthe *North pole,* 18. have the days and nights 6 months long.

Infinite *Islands* float in the Seas.

Distribuitur in *Zonas* V, quarum duae, *frigidae,* 9...9. sunt inhabitabiles; duae *Temperatae,* 10...10. & *Torrida,* 11. habitantur.

Ceterum divisa est in tres Continentes; nostram, 12. quae subdividitur in *Europam,* 13. *Asiam,* 14. & *Africam,* 15. in *Americam,* 16...16. (cujus incolae sunt *Antipodes* nobis;) & in *Terram Australem,* 17...17. adhuc incognitam. Habitantes sub *Arcto,* 18. habent Dies Noctes semestrales,

Infinitae *Insulae* natant in maribus.

Europe. - CVIII. - Europa.

The chief *Kingdoms* of *Europe,* are *Spain,* 1. *France,* 2. *Italy,* 3. *England,* 4. *Scotland,* 5. *Ireland,* 6. *Germany,* 7. *Bohemia,* 8. *Hungary,* 9. *Croatia,* 10. *Dacia,* 11. *Sclavonia,* 12. *Greece,* 13. *Thrace,* 14. *Podolia,* 15. *Tartary,* 16. *Lituania,* 17. *Poland,* 18. *The Netherlands,* 19. *Denmark,* 20. *Norway,* 21. *Swethland,* 22. *Lapland,* 23. *Finland,* 24. *Lisland,* 25. *Prussia,* 26, *Muscovy,* 27. and *Russia,* 28.

In *Europâ* nostrâ sunt *Regna* primaria, *Hispania,* 1. *Gallia,* 2. *Itulia,* 3. *Anglia* (Britania), 4. *Scotia,* 5. *Hibernia,* 6. *Germania,* 7. *Bohemia,* 8. *Hungaria,* 9. *Croatia,* 10. *Dacia,* 11. *Sclavonia,* 12. *Graecia,* 13. *Thracia,* 14. *Podolia,* 15. *Tartaria,* 16. *Lituania,* 17. *Polonia,* 18. *Belgium,* 19. *Dania,* 20. *Norvegia,* 21. *Suecia,* 22. *Lappia,* 23. *Finnia,* 24. *Livonia,* 25. *Borussia,* 26. *Muscovia,* 27. *Russia,* 28.

Moral Philosophy, - CIX. - Ethica.

This *Life* is a *way,* or a *place divided into two ways,* like *Pythagoras's Letter* Y. broad, 1. on the left hand track; narrow, 2. on the right; that belongs to *Vice,* 3. this to *Vertue,* 4.

Mind, Young Man, 5. imitate *Hercules:* leave the left hand way, turn from Vice; the *Entrance,* 6. is fair, but the *End,* 7. is ugly and steep down.

Go on the right hand, though it be thorny, 8. no way is unpassible to vertue; follow whither vertue leadeth through *narrow places* to *stately palaces,* to the *Tower of honour,* 9.

Keep the middle and straight *path,* and thou shalt go very safe.

Take heed thou do not go too much on the right hand, 10.

Bridle in, 12. the wild Horse, 11. of Affection, lest thou fall down headlong.

See thou dost not go amiss on the left hand, 13. in an ass-like sluggishness, 14. but go onwards constantly, persevere to the end, and thou shalt be crown'd, 15.

Vita haec est *via,* sive *Bivium,* simile Litterae *Pithagoricae* Y. latum, 1. sinistro tramite angustum, 2. dextro; ille *Vitii,* 3. est hic *Virtutis,* 4.

Adverte juvenis, 5. imitare *Herculem;* linque sinistram, aversare Vitium; *Aditus* speciosus, 6. sed *Exitus,* 7. turpis & praeceps.

Dextera ingredere, utut spinosa, 8. nulla via invia virtuti; sequere quâ viâ ducit virtus per *angusta,* ad *augusta,* ad *Arcem honoris,* 9. Tene medium & rectum *tramitem;* ibis tutissimus. Cave excedas ad dextram, 10.

Compesce freno, 12. equum ferocem, 11, Affectûs ne praeceps fias.

Cave deficias ad sinistram, 13. segnitie asininâ, 14. sed progredere constanter pertende ad finem, & coronaberis, 15.

Prudence. - CX. - Prudentia.

Prudence, 1. looketh upon all things as a *Serpent,* 2. and doeth, speaketh, or thinketh nothing in vain.

She *looks backwards,* 3. as into a *Looking-glass,* 4. to *things past;* and seeth *before her,* 5. as with a *Perspective-glass,* 7. *things to come,* or the *End,* 6. and so she perceiveth what she hath done, and what remaineth to be done.

She proposeth an *Honest, Profitable* and withal, if it may be done, a *Pleasant End,* to her Actions.

Having foreseen the *End,* she looketh out *Means,* as a *Way,* 8. which leadeth to the End; but such as are certain and easie, and fewer rather than more, lest anything should hinder.

She watcheth *Opportunity,* 9. (which having a *bushy fore-head,* 10. and being *bald-pated,* 11. and moreover having *wings,* 12. doth quickly slip away,) and catcheth it.

She goeth on her way warily, for fear she should stumble or go amiss.

Prudentia, 1. circumspectat omnia ut *Serpens,* 2. agitque, loquitur, aut cogitat nihil incassum.

Respicit, 3. tanquam in *Speculum,* 4. ad *praeterita;* & *prospicit,* 5. tanquam *Telescopio,* 7. *Futura,* seu *Finem,* 6. atque ita perspicit quid egerit, & quid restet agendum.

Actionibus suis praefigit *Scopum, Honestum, Utilem,* simulque, si fieri potest, *Jucundum.*

Fine prospecto, dispicit *Media,* ceu *Viam,* 8. quae ducit ad finem, sed certa & facilia; pauciora potiùs quàm plura, ne quid impediat.

Attendit *Occasioni,* 9. (quae *Fronte Capillata,* 10. sed vertice *calva,* 11. adhaec *alata,* 12. facile elabitur) eamque captat.

In viâ pergit cautè (providè) ne impingat aut aberret.

Diligence - CXI. - Sedulitas.

Diligence, 1. loveth labours, avoideth *Sloth,* is always at work, like the *Pismire,* 2. and carrieth together, as she doth, for herself, *Store* of all things, 3.

She doth not always sleep, or make holidays, as the *Sluggard,* 4. and the *Grashopper,* 5. do, whom *Want,* 6. at the last overtaketh.

Shepursueth what things she hath undertaken chearfully, even to the end; she putteth nothing off till the morrow, nor doth she sing the *Crow's* song, 7. which saith over and over, *Cras, Cras.*

After *labours undergone,* and ended, being even wearied, she resteth her self; but being refreshed with Rest, that she may not use her self to *Idleness,* she falleth again to her *Business.*

A diligent *Scholar* is like *Bees,* 8. which carry honey from divers *Flowers,* 9. into their *Hive,* 10.

Sedulitas, 1. amat labors, fugit *Ignaviam,* semper est in *opere,* ut *Formica,* 2. & comportat, ut ilia, sibi, omnium rerum *Copiam,* 3.

Non semper dormit, ferias agit, aut ut *Ignavus,* 4. & *Cicada,* 5. quos *Inopia,* 6. tandem premit.

Urget incepta alacriter ad finem usque; procrastinat nihil, nee cantat cantilenam *Corvi,* 7. qui ingeminat *Cras, Cras,*

Post *labores exantlatos,* & lassata, quiescit; sed recreata *Quiete,* ne adsuescat *Otio,* redit ad *Negotia.*

Diligens *Discipulus,* similis est *Apibus,* 8. qui congerunt mel ex variis *Floribus,* 9. in *Alveare* suum, 10.

Temperance. - CXII. - Temperantia.

Temperance, 1. prescribeth a mean to *meat* and *drink,* 2. and restraineth the *desire,* as with a *Bridle,* 3. and so moderateth all things, lest any thing too much be done.

Revellers are made *drunk,* 4. they *stumble,* 5. they *spue,* 6. and *babble,* 7.

From *Drunkenness* proceedeth *Lasciviousness;* from this a *lewd Life* amongst *Whoremasters,* 8. and *Whores,* 9. in *kissing, touching, embracing,* and *dancing,* 10.

Temperantia, 1. Praescribit *modum Cibo* & *Potui,* 2. & continet *cupidinem,* ecu *Freno,* 3. & sic moderator omnia ne quid nimis fiat.

Heluones (ganeones) *inebriantur,* 4. *titubant,* 5. *ructant* (vomunt), 6. & *rixantur,* 7.

E *Crapula* oritur *Lascivia;* ex hâc *Vita libidinosa* inter *Fornicatores,* 8. & *Scorta,* 9. *osculando* (basiando), *palpando, amplexando,* & *tripudiando,* 10.

Fortitude. - CXIII. - Fortitudo.

Fortitude, 1. is undaunted in adversity, and bold as a *Lion,* 2. but not haughty in Prosperity, leaning on her own *Pillar,* 3. *Constancy,* and being the same in all things, ready to undergo both *estates* with an even mind.

She receiveth the strokes of *Misfortune* with the *Shield,* 4. of *Sufferance:* and keepeth off the *Passions,* the enemies of quietness with the *Sword,* 5. of *Valour.*

Fortitudo, 1. impavida est in adversis, & confidens ut *Leo,* 2. at non tumida in Secundis, innixa suo *Columini,* 3. *Constantiae;* & eadem in omnibus, parata ad ferendam utramque *fortunam* aequo animo.

Excipit ictus *Infortunii Clypeo,* 4. *Tolerantiae:* & propellit *Affectus,* hostes Euthymiae *gladio,* 5. *Virtutis.*

Patience. - CXIV. - Patientia.

Patience, 1. endureth *Calamities,* 2. and *Wrongs,* 3. meekly like a *Lamb,* 4. as the Fatherly *chastisement of God,* 5.

In the meanwhile she leaneth upon the *Anchor of Hope,* 6. (as a *Ship,* 7. tossed by waves in the Sea) *she prayeth to God,* 8. weeping, and expecteth the *Sun,* 10. after *cloudy weather,* 9. suffering evils, and hoping better things.

On the contrary, the *impatient person,* 11. waileth, lamenteth, *rageth against himself,* 12. grumbleth like a *Dog,* 13. and yet doth no good; at the last he despaireth, and becometh *his own Murtherer,* 14.

Being full of rage he desireth to revenge wrongs.

Patientia, 1. tolerat *Calamitates,* 2. & *Injurias,* 3. humiliter ut *Agnus,* 4. tanquam paternam *ferulam Dei,* 5.

Interim innititur *Spei Anchorae,* 6. (ut *Navis,* 7. fluctuans mari) *Deo supplicat,* 8. illacrymando, & expectat *Phoebum,* 10. post *Nubila,* 9. ferens mala, sperans meliora.

Contra, *Impatiens,* 11. plorat, lamentatur, *debacchatur,* 12. *in seipsum,* obmurmurat ut *Canis,* 13. & tamen nil proficit; tandem desperat, & fit *Autochir,* 14. Furibundus cupit vindicare injurias.

Humanity. - CXV. - Humanitas.

Men are made for one another's *good;* therefore let them be *kind.* Be thou sweet and lovely in thy *Countenance,* 1. gentle and civil in thy *Behaviour* and *Manners,* 2. affable and true spoken with thy *Mouth,* 3. affectionate and *candid* in thy *Heart,* 4.

So love, and so shalt thou be loved; and there will be a mutual *Friendship,* 5. as that of *Turtle-doves,* 6. hearty, gentle, and wishing well on both parts.

Froward Men are hateful, teasty, unpleasant, contentious, *angry,* 7. *cruel,* 8. and implacable, (rather Wolves and Lions, than Men) and such as fall out among themselves, hereupon they fight in a *Duel,* 9. *Envy,* 10. wishing ill to others, pineth away her self.

Homines facti sunt ad mutua *commoda;* ergò sint *humani.*

Sis suavis & amabilis *Vultu,* 1. comis & urbanus *Gestu* ac *Moribus,* 2. affabilis & verax. *Ore,* 3. candens & *candidus Corde,* 4.

Sic ama, sic amaberis; & fiat mutua *Amicitia,* 5. ceu *Turturum,* 6. concors, mansueta, & benevola utrinque.

Morosi homines, sunt odiosi, torvi, illepidi. contentiosi, *iracundi,* 7. *crudeles,* 8. ac implacabiles, (magis Lupi & Leones, quàm homines) & inter se discordes, hinc confligunt *Duelle,* 9. *Invidia,* 10. malè cupiendo aliis, conficit seipsam.

Justice. - CXVI. - Justitia.

Justice, 1. is painted, sitting on a *square stone,* 2. for she ought to be immoveable; with *hood-winked eyes,* 3. that she may not respect persons; *stopping the left ear,* 4. to be reserved for the other party; Holding in her right Hand a *Sword,* 5. and a *Bridle,* 6. to punish and restrain evil men;

Besides, *a pair of Balances,* 7 . in the *right Scale,* 8, whereof *Deserts,* and in the *left,* 9. *Rewards* being put, are made even one with another, and so good Men are incited to virtue, as it were with *Spurs,* 10.

In *Bargains,* 11. let Men deal candidly, let them stand to their *Covenants* and *Promises;* let *that which is given one to keep,* and *that which is lent,* be restored: let no man be *pillaged,* 12. or *hurt,* 13. let every one have his own: these are the precepts of Justice.

Such things as these are forbidden in *God's* 5*th.* and 7*th. Commandment,* and deservedly punish'd on the *Gallows* and the *Wheel,* 14.

Justitia, 1. pingitur, sedens in *lapide quadrato,* 2. nam decet esse immobilis; *obvelatis oculis,* 3. ad non respiciendum personas; *claudens aurem sinistram,* 4. reservandam alteri parti; Tenens dextrâ *Gladium,* 5. & *Froenum,* 6. ad puniendum & coërcendum malos;

Praeterea, *Stateram,* 7. cujus *dextrae Lanci,* 8. *Merita, Sinistrae,* 9. *Praemia* imposita, sibi invicem exequantur, atque ita boni incitantur ad virtutem, ceu *Calcaribus,* 10.

In *Contractibus,* 11. candidè agatur: stetur *Pactis* & *Promissis; Depositum,* & *Mutuum,* reddantur: nemo *expiletur,* 12. aut *loedatur,* 13. suum cuique tribuatur: haec sunt praecepta Justitiae.

Talio prohibentur, *quinto* & *septimo Dei Praecepto,* & merito puniuntur *Cruce* ac *Rotâ,* 14.

Liberality. - CXVII. - Liberalitas.

Liberality, 1. keepeth a mean about *Riches,* which she honestly seeketh, that she may have somewhat to bestow on them that *want,* 2.

She *cloatheth,* 3. *nourisheth,* 4. and *enricheth,* 5. these with a *chearful countenance,* 6. and a *winged hand,* 7.

She submitteth her *wealth,* 8. to her self, not her self to it, as the *covetous man,* 9. doth, who hath, that he may have, and is not the *Owner,* but the *Keeper* of his goods, and being unsatiable, always *scrapeth together,* 10. with his Nails. Moreover he spareth and keepeth, *hoarding up,* 11. that he may always have.

But the *Prodigal,* 12. badly spendeth things well gotten, and at the last wanteth.

Liberalitas, 1. servat modum circa *Divitias,* quas honestè quaerit ut habeat quod largiatur *Egenis,* 2.

Hos *vestit,* 3. *nutrit,* 4. *ditat,* 5. *Vultu hilari,* 6. & *Manu alatâ,* 7.

Subjicit *opes,* 8. sibi, non se illis, ut *Avarus,* 9. qui habet, ut habeat, & non est *Possessor* sed *Custos* bonorum suorum, & insatiabilis, semper *corradit,* 10. Unguibus suis.

Sed & parcit & adservat, *occludendo,* 11. ut semper habeat.

At *Prodigus,* 12. malè disperdit benè parta, ac tandem eget.

Society betwixt Man and Wife. - CXVIII. - Societas Conjugalis.

Marriage was appointed by God in Paradise, for mutual *help,* and the *Propagation* of mankind.

A young man (*a single man*) being to be married, should be furnished either with *Wealth,* or a *Trade* and *Science,* which may serve for getting a living; that he may be able to maintain a *Family.*

Then he chooseth himself a *Maid* that is *Marriageable,* (or a *Widow*) whom he loveth; nevertheless a greater Regard is to be had of *Virtue,* and *Honesty,* than of *Beauty* or *Portion.*

Afterwards, he doth not betroth her to himself closely, but entreateth for her as a *Woer,* first to the *Father,* 1. and then the *Mother,* 2. or the *Guardians,* or *Kinsfolks,* by such *as help to make the match,* 3.

When she is espous'd to him, he becometh the *Bridegroom,* 4. and she the *Bride,* 5. and the *Contract* is made, and an *Instrument of Dowry,* 6. is written.

At the last the *Wedding* is made, where they are joined together by the *Priest,* 7. giving their *Hands,* 8. one to another, and *Wedding-rings,* 9. then they feast with the witnesses that are invited.

After this they are called *Husband* and *Wife;* when she is dead he becometh a *Widower.*

Matrimonium institutum est à Deo in Paradiso, ad mutuum *adjutorium,* & *propagationem,* generis humani.

Vir Juvenis (*Coelebs*) conjugium initurus, instructus sit aut *Opibus,* aut *Arte* & *Scientiâ,* quae sit de pane lucrando; ut possit sustentare *Familiam.*

Deinde eligit sibi *Virginem Nubilem,* (aut *Viduam*) quam adamat; ubi tamen major ratio habenda *Virtutis* & *Honestatis,* quàm *Formae* aut *Dotis.*

Posthaec, non clam despondet sibi eam, sed ambit, ut *Procus,* apud *Patrem,* 1. & *Matrem,* 2. vel apud *Tutores,* & *Cognatos,* per *Pronubos,* 3.

Eâ sibi desponsâ, fit *Sponsus,* 4. & ipsa *Sponsa,* 5, fiuntque *Sponsalia,* & scribitur *Instrumentum Dotale,* 6.

Tandem fiunt *Nuptiae* ubi copulantur à *Sacerdote,* 7. datis *Manibus,* 8. ultrò citroque, & *Annulis Nuptialibus,* 9. tum epulantur cum invitatis testibus.

Abhinc dicuntur *Maritus* & *Uxor;* hâc mortuâ ille fit *Viduus.*

The Tree of Consanguinity. - CXIX. - Arbor Consanguinitatis.

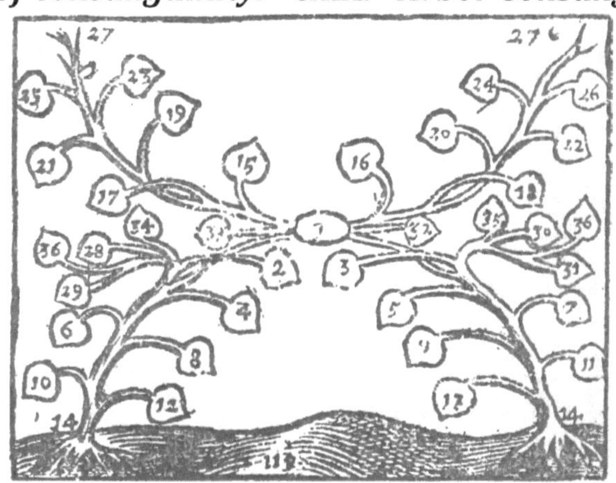

In *Consanguinity* there touch a *Man,* 1. in *Lineal Ascent,* the *Father* (the Father-in-law), 2. and the *Mother* (the *Mother-in-law*), 3. the *Grandfather,* 4. and the *Grandmother,* 5. the *Great Grandfather,* 6. and the *Great Grandmother,* 7. the *great great Grandfather,* 8. the *great great Grandmother,* 9. the *great great Grandfather's Father,* 10. the *great great Grandmother's Mother,* 11. the *great great Grandfather's Grandfather,* 12. the *great great Grandmother's Grandmother,* 13.

Those beyond these are called *Ancestors,* 14...14.

In a *Lineal descent,* the *Son* (*the son-in-law*), 15, and the *Daughter,* (the Daughter-in-law), 16, the *Nephew,* 17. and the *Neece,* 18. the *Nephews Son,* 19. and the *Nephew's Daughter,* 20. the *Nephew's Nephew,* 21. and the *Neece's Neece,* 22. the *Nephew's Nephew's Son,* 23. the *Neece's Neece's Daughter,* 24. the *Nephew's Nephew's Nephew,* 25. the *Neece's Neece's Neece,* 26. Those beyond these are called *Posterity,* 27...27.

In a *Collateral Line* are the *Uncle by the Fathers side,* 28. and *the Aunt by the Fathers side,* 29. the *Uncle by the Mothers side,* 30. and the *Aunt by the Mothers side,* 3 1 . the *Brother,* 32. and the *Sister,* 33. the *Brothers Son,* 34. the *Sisters Son,* 35. and the *Cousin by the Brother* and *Sister,* 36.

Hominem, 1. *Consanguinitate* attingunt, in Linea *ascendenti, Pater* (*Vitricus*), 2. & *Mater* (*Noverca*), 3. *Avus,* 4. *Avia,* 5. *Proavus,* 6. & *Proavia,* 7. *Adavus,* 8. & *Abavia,* 9. *Atavus,* 10. & *Atavia,* 11. *Tritavus,* 12. & *Tritavia,* 13.

Ulteriores dicuntur *Majores,* 14...14. In *Linea descendenti, Filius* (*Privignus*), 15. & *Filia* (*Privigna*), 16. *Nepos,* 17. & *Neptis,* 18. *Pronepos,* 19. & *Proneptis,*

26. *Abnepos,* 21. & *Abneptis,* 22. *Atnepos,* 23. & *Atneptis,* 24. *Trinepos,* 25. & *Trineptis,* 26. Ulteriores dicuntur *Posteri,* 27...27.

In *Linea Collaterali* sunt *Patruus,* 28. & *Amita,* 29. *Avunculus,* 30. & *Malertera,* 31. *Frater,* 32. & *Soror,* 33. *Patruelis,* 34. *Sobrinus, 35.* & *Amitinus,* 36.

The Society betwixt Parents and Children. - CXX. - Societas Parentalis.

Married Persons, (by the blessing of God) have *Issue,* and become *Parents,*

The *Father,* 1. begetteth and the *Mother,* 2. beareth *Sons,* 3. and *Daughters,* 4. (sometimes *Twins*).

The *Infant,* 5. is wrapped in *Swadling-cloathes,* 6. is laid in a *Cradle,* 7. is suckled by the Mother with her *Breasts,* 8. and fed with *Pap,* 9.

Afterwards it learneth to go by a *Standing-stool,* 10. playeth with *Rattles,* 11. and beginneth to speak.

As it beginneth to grow older, it is accustomed to *Piety,* 12. and *Labour,* 13. and is chastised, 14. if it be not dutiful.

Children owe to Parents Reverence and Service.

The Father maintaineth his Children *by taking pains,* 15.

Conjuges, (ex benedictione Dei) suscipiunt *Sobolem* (Prolem) & fiunt *Parentes.*

Pater, 1. generat & *Mater,* 2. parit *Filios,* 3. & *Filias,* 4. (aliquando *Gemellos*).

Infans, 5. involvitur *Fasciis,* 6. reponitur in *Cunas,* 7. lactatur a matre *Uberibus, 8.* & nutritur *Pappis,* 9. Deinde discit incedere *Seperasto,* 10. ludit *Crepundiis,* 11. & incipit fari. Crescente aetate, adsuescit *Pietati,* 12. & *Labori,* 13. & castigatur, 14. si non sit morigerus.

Liberi debent Parentibus Cultum & Officium.

Pater sustentat Liberos, *laborando,* 15.

The Society betwixt Masters and Servants. - CXXI. - Societas herilis.

The *Master* (*the goodman of the House*) 1. hath *Men-servants,* 2. the *Mistress* (*the good wife of the House*), 3. *Maidens,* 4.

They appoint these their *Work,* 6. and divide *them their tasks,* 5. which are faithfully to be done by them without murmuring and loss: for which their *Wages,* and *Meat* and *Drink* is allowed them.

A *Servant* was heretofore a *Slave,* over whom the Master had power of life and death.

At this day the poorer sort serve in a free manner,being hired for Wages.

Herus (*Pater familias*), 1. habet *Famulos* (*Servos*), 2.

Hera (*Mater familias*), 3. *Ancillas,* 4.

Illi mandant his *Opera,* 6. & distribuunt *Laborum Pensa,* 5. qua ab his fideliter sunt exsequenda sine murmure & dispendio; pro quo *Merces* & *Alimonia* praebentur ipsis.

Servus olim erat *Mancipium,* in quem Domino potestas fuit vitae & necis

Hodiè pauperiores serviunt liberè, conducti mercede.

A City. - CXXII. – Urbs.

Of many Houses is made a *Village,* 1. or a *Town,* or a *City,* 2.

That and this are fenced and begirt with a *Wall,* 3. a *Trench,* 4. *Bulwarks,* 5. and *Pallisadoes,* 6.

Within the Walls is the *void Place,* 7 . without, the *Ditch,* 8.

In the Walls are *Fortresses,* 9. and *Towers,* 10. *Watch-Towers,* 11. are upon the higher places.

The entrance into a City is made out of the *Suburbs,* 12. through *Gates,* 13. over the *Bridge,* 14.

The *Gate* hath a *Portcullis,* 15. a *Draw-bridge,* 16. *two-leaved Doors,* 17. *Locks* and *Bolts,* as also *Barrs,* 18.

In the Suburbs are *Gardens,* 19. and *Garden-houses,* 20. and also *Burying-places,* 21.

Ex multis Domibus fit *Pagus,* 1. vel *Oppidum,* vel *Urbs,* 2.

Istud & hsec muniuntur & cinguntur *Moenibus* (*Muro*), 3. *Vallo,* 4. *Aggeribus,* 5. & *Vallis,* 6.

Intra muros est *Pomoerium,* 7. extrà, *Fossa,* 8.

In moenibus sunt *Propugnacula,* 9. & *Turres,* 10. *Specula,* 11. extant in editioribus locis.

Ingressus in Urbem fit ex *Suburbio,* 2. per *Portam,* 13. super *Pontem,* 14.

Porta habet *Cataractas,* 15. *Pontem versatilem,* 16. *Valvas,* 17.

Claustra & *Repagula,* ut & *Vectes,* 18.

In Suburbiis sunt *Horti,* 19. & *Suburbana,* 20. ut & *Caemeteria,* 21.

The inward parts of a City - CXXIII. - Interiora Urbis.

Within the City are *Streets,* 1. paved with Stones; *Market-places,* 2. (in some places with *Galleries*), 3. and *narrow Lanes,* 4.

The Publick Buildings are in the middle of the City, the *Church,* 5. the *School,* 6. the *Guild-Hall,* 7, the *Exchange,* 8.

About thc Walls and the Gates are the *Magazine,* 9. the *Granary,* 10. *Inns, Ale-houses, Cooks-shops,* 11. the *Play-house,* 12. and the *Spittle,* 13.

In the by-places are *Houses of Office,* 14. and the *Prison,* 15.

In the chief Steeple is the *Clock,* 16. and the *Watchmans* Dwelling, 17.

In the Streets are *Wells,* 18.

The *River,* 19. or *Beck,* runneth about the City, serveth to wash away the *filth.* The *Tower,* 20. standeth in the highest part of the City.

Intra urbem sunt *Platece* (Vici), 1. stratse Lapidibus; *Fora,* 2. (alicubi cum *Porticibus*), 3. & *Angiportus,* 4. Publica aedificia sunt in medio Urbis, *Templum,* 5. *Schola,* 6. *Curia,* 7. *Domus Mercaturae,* 8. Circa Moenia, & Portas *Armamentarium,* 9. *Granarium,* 10. *Diversoria, Popinae,* & *Cauponae,* 11.

Theatrum, 12. *Nosodochium,* 13. In recessibus, *Foricae* (Cloacae), 14. & *Custodia* (Career), In turre primariâ est *Horologium,* 16. & habitatio *Vigilum,* 17. In Plateis sunt *Putei,* 18. *Fluvius,* 19. vel *Rivus,* interfluens Urbem, inservit eluendis *sordibus. Arx,* 20. extat in summo Urbis.

Judgment. - CXXIV. - Judicium.

The best Law, is a quiet *agreement,* made either by themselves. betwixt whom the sute is, or by an *Umpire.*

If this do not proceed, they come into *Court,* 1. (heretofore they judg'd in the Market-place; at this day in the *Moot-hall*) in which the *Judge,* 2. sitteth with his *Assessors,* 3. the *Clerk,* 4. taketh their Votes in writing.

The *Plaintiff,* 5. accuseth the *Defendant,* 6. and produceth *Witnesses,* 7. against him.

The *Defendant* excuseth himself by a *Counsellor,* 8. whom the Plaintiffs *Counsellor,* 9. contradicts.

Then the *Judge* pronounceth *Sentence,* acquitting the *innocent,* and condemning him that is *guilty,* to a *Punishment,* or a *Fine,* or *Torment.*

Optimum Jus, est placida *conventio,* facta vel ab ipsis, inter quos lis est vel ab *Arbitro.*

Haec si non procedit, venitur in *Forum,* 1. (olim judicabant in Foro, hodiè in *Praetorio*) cui *Judex* (Praetor), 2. praesidet cum *Assessoribus,* 3. *Dicographus,* 4. excipit Vota calamo.

Actor, 5. accusat *Reum,* 6. & producit *Testes,* 7. contra ilium.

Reus excusat se per *Advocatum,* 8. cui Actoris *Procurator,* 9. contradicit.

Tum *Judex Sententiam* pronunciat, absolvens *insontem,* & damnans *sontem* ad *Poenam,* vel *Mulctam,* vel ad *Supplicium.*

The Tormenting of Malefactors. - CXXV. - Supplicia Malefactorum.

Malefactors, 1. are brought from the *Prison,* 3. (where they are wont to be tortured) by *Serjeants,* 2. or dragged with a *Horse,* 15. to place of *Execution.*

Thieves, 4. are hanged by the *Hangman,* 6. on a *Gallows,* 5. *Whoremasters* are beheaded, 7.

Murtherers and *Robbers* are either laid upon a *Wheel,* 8. having their *Legs broken,* or fastened upon a *Stake,* 9.

Witches are burnt in a *great Fire,* 10.

Some before they are executed have their *Tongues cut out,* 11. or have their *Hand,* 12. cut off upon a *Block,* 13. or are burnt with *Pincers,* 14. They that have their Life given them, are set on the *Pillory,* 16, or *strapado'd,* 17. are set upon a *wooden Horse,* 18. have their *Ears cut off,* 19. are whipped with *Rods,* 20. are branded, are banished, are condemned to the *Gallies,* or to perpetual Imprisonment. *Traytors* are pull'd in pieces with four *Horses.*

Malefici, 1. producuntur, è *Carcere,* 3. (ubi torqueri solent) per *Lictores,* 2. vel *Equo raptantur,* 15. ad locum *Supplicii.*

Fures, 4. suspenduntura *Carnifice,* 6. in *Patibulo,* 5. *Moechi* decollantur, 7.

Homicidae. (Sicarii) ac *Latrones* (Piratae) vel imponuntur *Rotae crucifragio plexi,* 8. vel *Palo* infiguntur, 9.

Striges (Lamiae) cremantur super *Rogum,* 10.

Quidam antequam supplicio afficiantur *elinguantur,* 11. aut plectuntur *Manu,* 12. super *Cippum,* 13. aut *Forcipibus,* 14. uruntur Vitâ donati, constringuntur *Numellis,* 16. luxantur, 17. imponuntur *Equuleo,* 18. *truncantur Auribus,* 19, *coeduntur Virgis,* 20. Stigmate notantur, relegantur, damnantur ad *Triremes,* vel ad Carcerem perpetuum. *Perduelles* discerpuntur *Quadrigis.*

Merchandizing. – CXXVI. – Mercatura.

Wares brought from other places are either exchanged in an *Exchange,* 1. or exposed to sale in *Warehouses,* 2. and they are sold for *Money,* 3. being either measured with an *Eln,* 4. or weighed in a *pair of Balances,* 5.

Shop-keepers, 6. *Pedlars,* 7. and *Brokers,* 8. would also be called *Merchants,* 9.

The *Seller* braggeth of a thing that is to be sold, and setteth the rate of it, and how much it may be sold for.

The *Buyer,* 10. cheap neth and offereth the price.

If any one bid *against him,* 11. the thing is delivered to him that promiseth the most.

Merces, aliunde allatae, aliunde vel commutantur in *Domo Commerciorum,* 1. vel exponuntur venum in *Tabernis Mercimoniorum,* 2. & venduntur pro *Pecuniâ* (monetâ), 3. vel mensuratae *Ulnâ,* 4. vel ponderatae *Librâ,* 5.

Tabernarii. 6, *Circumforanei,* 7. & *Scrutarii,* 8. etiam volunt dici *Mercatores,* 9.

Venditor ostentat rem promercalem, & indicat pretium, quanti liceat. *Emptor,* 10. licetur, & pretium offert.

Si quis *contralicetur,* 11. ei res addicitur qui pollicetur plurimum.

Measures and Weights. - CXXVII. - Mensurae & Pondera.

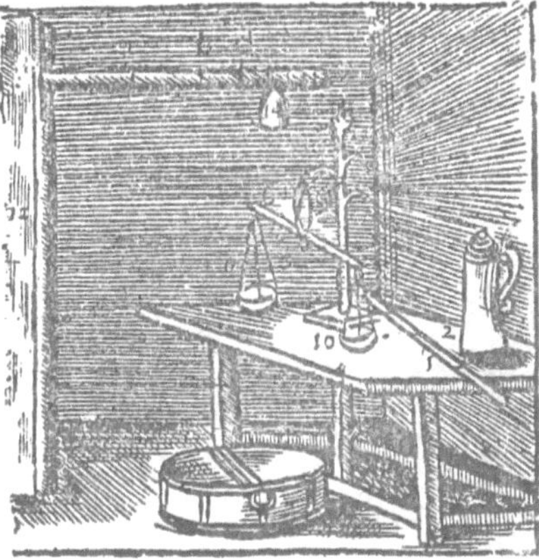

We measure things that hang together with an *Eln,* 1. liquid things with a *Gallon,* 2. and dry things by a *two-bushel Measure,* 3.

We try the heaviness of things by *Weights,* 4. and *Balances,* 5. the *Beam,* 6. in the midst whereof is a little *Axle-tree,* 7. above the *cheeks* and the *hole,* 8. in which the *Needle,* 9. moveth it self to and fro: on both sides are the Scales, 10. hanging by *little Cords,* 11. The *Brasiers balance,* 12. weigheth things by hanging them on a *Hook,* 13. and the *Weight,* 14. opposite to them which in (a) weigheth as much as the thing, in (b) twice so much in (c) thrice so much, &c.

Res continuas metimur *Ulnâ,* 1. liquidas *Congio,* 2. aridas *Medimno,* 3.

Gravitatem rerum experimur *Ponderibus,* 4. & *Librâ* (bilance), 5. In hâc primò est *Jugum* (Scapus), 6. in cujus medio *Axiculus,* 7. superius *trutina* & *agina,* 8. in quâ *Examen,* 9. sese agitat: utrinque sunt *Lances,* 10. pendentes *Funiculis,* 11. *Statera,* 12. ponderat res,suspendendo illas *Unco,* 13. & *Pondus,* 14. ex opposito, quod in (a) aequiponderat rei, in (b) bis tantum, in (c) ter, &c.

Physick - CXXVIII. - Ars Medica.

The *Patient,* 1. sendeth for a *Physician,* 2. who feeleth his *Pulse,* 3, and looketh upon his *Water,* 4. and then prescribeth a *Receipt* in a *Bill,* 5.

That is made ready by an *Apothecary,* 6. in a *Apothecaries Shop,* 7. where *Drugs* are kept in *Drawers,* 8. *Boxes,* 9. and *Gally-pots,* 10.

And it is either a *Potion,* 11. or *Powder,* 12. or *Pills,* 13. or *Trochisks,* 14. or an *Electuary,* 15. *Diet* and *Prayer,* 16. is the best *Physick.*

The *Chirurgeon,* 18. cureth *Wounds,* 17. and *Ulcers,* with *Plasters,* 19.

Aegrotans, 1. accersit *Medicum,* 2. qui tangit ipsius *Arteriam,* 3. & inspicit *Urinam,* 4. tum praescribit *Medicamentum* in *Schedula,* 5.

Istud paratur à *Pharmacopaeo,* 6. in *Pharmacopolio,* 7. ubi *Pharmaca* adservantur in *Capsulis,* 8. *Pyxidibus,* 9. & *Lagenis,* 10.

Estque vel *Potio,* 11. vel *Pulvis,* 12. vel *Pillulae,* 13. vel *Pastilli,* 14. vel *Electuarium,* 15.

Diaeta & *Oratio,* 16. est optima *Medicina,*

Chirurgus, 18. curat *Vulnera,* 17. & *Ulcera, Spleniis* (emplastris), 19.

A Burial. – CXXIX. - Sepultura.

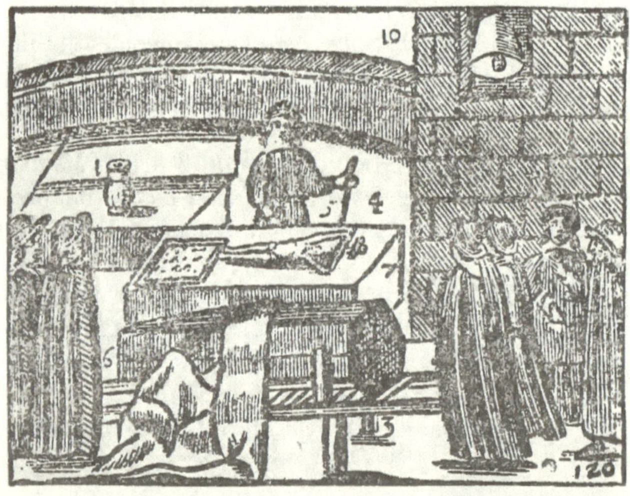

Dead Folks heretofore were burned, and their Ashes put into an *Urn,* 1.

We enclose our *dead Folks* in a *Coffin,* 2. lay them upon a *Bier,* 3. and see they be carried out in a *Funeral Pomp* towards the *Church-yard,* 4. where they are laid in a *Grave,* 6, by the *Bearers,* 5. and are interred; this is covered with a *Grave-stone,* 7. and is adorned with *Tombs,* 8. and *Epitaphs,* 9. As the Corps go along *Psalms* are sung-, and the *Bells* are rung, 10.

Defuncti olim cremabantur, & Cineres recondebantur in *Urna,* 1.

Nos includiaius nostros *Demortuos Loculo,* (*Capulo*), 2. imponimus *Feretro,* 3. & curamus efferri *Pompâ Funebri* versus *Coemeterium,* 4. ubi inferuntur,

Sepulchro, 6. a *Vespillonibus,* & humantur; hoc tegitur *Cippo,* 7. & ornatur *Monumentis,* 8. ac *Epitaphiis,* 9. Funere prodeunte, *Hymni* cantantur, & *Campanae,* 10. pulsantur.

A Stage-play. - CXXX. - Ludus Scenictis.

In a *Play-house,* 1. which is trimmed with *Hangings,* 2. and covered with *Curtains,* 3.) *Comcdics* and *Tragedies* are acted, wherein memorable things are represented; as here, the History of the *Prodigal Son,* 4. and his *Father,* 5. by whom he is entertain'd, being return'd home.

The *Players* act being in disguise; the *Fool,* 6. maketh Jests.

The chief of the Spectators sit in the *Gallery,* 7. the common sort stand on the *Ground,* 8. and clap the hands, if anything please them.

In *Theatro,* 1. (quod vestitur *Tapetibus,* 2. & tegitur *Sipariis,* 3.) *Comediae* vel *Tragoediae* aguntur, quibus repraesentantur res memorabiles ut hic, Historia de *Filio Prodigo,* 4. & *Pafre,* 5. ipsius, à quo recipitur, domum redux.

Actores (*Histriones*) agunt personati; *Morio,* 6. dat Jocos.

Spectatorum primarii, sedent in *Orchestra,* 7. plebs Stat in *Cavea,* 8. & plaudit, si quid arridet.

Sleights. - CXXXI. - Praestigiae.

The *Tumbler,* 1. maketh several *Shows* by the nimbleness of his body, walking to and fro on his hands, leaping through a *Hoop,* 2. &c.

Sometimes also he *danceth,* 4. having on a Vizzard.

The *Jugler,* 3. sheweth *sleights,* out of a *Purse.*

The *Rope-dancer,* 5. goeth and danceth upon a *Rope,* holdeth a *Poise,* 6. in his hand; or hangeth himself by the *hand* or *foot,* 7. &c.

Praestigiator, 1. facit varia *Spectacula,* volubilitate corporis, deambulando *manibus,* saliendo per *Circulum,* 2. &c.

Interdum etiam *tripudiat,* 4. Larvatus. *Agyrta,* 3. facit *praestigias* è *Marsupio. Funambulus,* 5. graditur & saltat super *Funem,* tenens *Halterem,* 6. manu; aut suspendit se *manu* vel *pede,* 7. &c.

The Fencing-School. – CXXXII. - Palestra.

Fencers meet in a Duel in a *Fencing-place,* fighting with *Swords,* 1. or *Pikes,* 2. and *Halberds,* 3. or *Short-swords,* 4. or *Rapiers,* 5. *having balls at the point* (lest they wound one another mortally) or with *two edged-Swords* and a *Dagger,* 6. together.

Wrestlers, 7. (among the Romans in time past were nayked and anointed with Oyl) take hold of one another and strive whether can throw the other, especially by *tripping up his heels,* 8.

Hood-winked Fencers, 9. fought with their fists in a ridiculous strife, to wit, with their Eyes coverered.

Pugiles congrediuntur Duello in *Palestra,* decertantes vel *Gladiis,* 1. vel *Hastilibus,* 2. & *Bipennibus,* 3. vel *Semispathis,* 4. vel *Ensibus,* 5. *mucronem obligatis,* (ne laedet lethaliter) vel *Frameis* & *Pugione,* 6, simul.

Luctatores, 7. (apud Romanos olim nudi & inuncti Oleo) prehendunt se invicem & annituntur uter alterum prosternere possit, praeprimis *supplantando,* 8.

Andabatae, 9, pugnabant pugnis ridiculo certamine, nimirum Oculis obvelatis.

Tennis-play. - CXXXIII. - Ludus Pilae.

In a *Tennis Court,* 1. they play with a *Ball,* 2. which one throweth, and another taketh, and sendeth it back with a *Racket,* 3. and that is the Sport of Noble Men to stir their Body.

A *Wind-ball,* 4. being filled with Air, by means of a *Ventil,* is tossed to and fro with the *Fist,* 5. in the open Air.

In *Sphaeristerio,* 1. luditur *Pilâ,* 2. quam alter mittit, alter excipit, & remittit *Reticulo,* 3. idque est Lusus Nobilium ad commotionem Corporis. *Follis* (pila magna), 4. distenta Aere ope *Epistomii,* reverberberatur *Pugno,* 5. sub Dio.

Dice-play - CXXXIV. - Ludus Aleae.

We play with *Dice,* 1. either they that throw the most *take up all;* or we throw them through a *Casting-box,* 2. upon a *Board,* 3. marked with figures, and this is *Dice-players game* at *casting Lots.*

Men play by *Luck* and *Skill* at *Tables.* in a pair of *Tables,* 4. and at *Cards,* 5.

We play at *Chesse* on a *Chesse-board,* 6. where only art beareth the sway.

The most ingenious Game is the Game of *Chesse,* 7. wherein as it were two Armies fight together in Battel.

Tesseris (*talis*), 1. ludimus vel *Plistobolindam;* vel immittimus illas per *Frittillum,* 2. in *Tabellam,* 3. notatam numeris, idque est *Ludas Sortilegii Aleatorum. Sorte* & *Arte* luditur *Calculis* in *Alveo aleatorio,* 4. & *Chartis lusoriis,* 5. Ludimus *Abaculis* in *Abaco,* 6. ubi sola ars regnat.

Ingeniosissimus Ludus est Ludus *Latrunculorum,* 7. quo veluti duo Exercitus confligunt Praelio.

Races. - CXXXV. - Cursus Certamina.

Boys exercise themselves by running, either upon the *Ice,* 1. in *Scrick-shoes,* 2. where they are carried also upon *Sleds,* 3. or in the open Field, making a *Line,* 4. which he that desireth to win, ought to touch, but not to run beyond it. Heretofore *Runners,* 5. run betwixt *Rails,* 6. to the *Goal,* 7. and he that toucheth it first receiveth the *Prize,* 8. *from him that gave the prize,* 9.

At this day *Tilting* (or the quintain) is used, (where a *Hoop,* 11. is struck at with a *Truncheon,* 10.) instead of *Horse-races,* which are grown out of use.

Pueri exercent se cursu, sive super *Glaciem,* 1. *Diabatris,* 2. ubi etiam vehuntur *Trahis,* 3. sive in Campo, designantes *Lineam,* 4. quam qui vincere cupit debet attingere, at non ultrâ procurrere. Olim decurrebant *Cursores,* 5. inter *Cancellos,* 6. ad *Metam,* 7. & qui primum contingebat eam, accipiebat *Brabeum,* (*praemium*), 8. à *Brabeuta,* 9.

Hodie *Hastiludia* habentur, (ubi *Circulus,* 11. petitur *Lancea,* 10.) loco *Equiriorum,* quae abierunt in desuetudinem.

Boys Sport. - CXXXVI. - Ludi Pueriles.

Boys use to play either with *Bowling-stones* 1. or throwing a *Bowl,* 2. at *Nine-pins,* 3. or striking a *Ball,* through a *Ring,* 5. with a *Bandy,* 4. or scourging a *Top,* 6. with a *Whip,* 7. or shooting with a *Trunk,* 8. and a *Bow,* 9. or going upon *Stilts,* 10. or tossing and swinging themselves upon a *Merry-totter,* 11.

Pueri solert ludere vel *Globis fictilibus,* 1. vel jactantes *Globum,* 2. ad *Conas,* 3. vel mittentes *Sphaerulam* per *Annulum,* 5. *Clava,* 4. versantes *Turbinem,* 6. *Flagello,* 7. vel jaculantes *Sclopo,* 8. & *Arcu,* 9. vel incidentes *Grallis,* 10. vel super *Petaurum,* 11. se agitantes & oscillantes.

The Kingdom and the Region. - CXXXVII. – Regnum & Regio.

Many *Cities* and *Villages* make a *Region* and a *Kingdom.*

The *King* or *Prince* resideth in the *chief City,* 1. the *Noblemen, Lords,* and *Earls* dwell in the *Castles,* 2. that lie about it; the *Country People* dwell in *Villages,* 3. He hath his *toll-places* upon *navigable Rivers,* 4. and *high-Roads,* 5. where *Portage* and *Tollage* is exacted of them that sail or travel.

Multae *Urbes* & *Pagi* faciunt *Regionem* & *Regnum.*

Rex aut *Princeps* sedet in *Metropoli,* 1. *Nobiles, Barones,* & *Comites* habitant in *Arcibus,* 2. circumjacentibus; *Rustici* in *Pagis,* 3.

Habet *telonia sua* juxta *Flumina navigabilia,* 4. & *Vias regias,* 5. ubi *Portorum* & *Vectigal* exigitur a navigantibus & iter facientibus.

Regal Majesty. - CXXXVIII. - Regia Majestas.

The King, 1. sitteth on his Throne, 2. in Kingly State, with a stately Habit, 3. crowned with a Diadejn, 4. holding a Scepter, 5. in his Hand, being attended with a Company of Courtiers.

The chief among these, are the Chancellor, 6. with the Counsellors and Secretaries, the Lord-mar shall, 7. the Comptroller, 8. the Cup-bearer, 9. the Taster, 10. the Treasurer, 11, the ,/,/z Chamberlain, 12. and the Master of the Morse, 13.

There are subordinate to these the Noble Courtiers, 14. the Noble Pages, 15 . with the Chamberlains, and Lacquies, 16. the Guard, 17, with their Attendance.

He solemnly giveth Audience to the Ambassadors of Foreign Princes, 18.

He sendeth his Vice-gerents, Deputies, Governors, Treasurers, and Ambassadors to other places, to whom he sendeth new Commissions ever and anon by the Posts, 19.

The Pool, 20. maketh Laughter by his toysom Actions.

Rex, 1. sedet in suo Solio, 2. in regio splendore, magnifico Habitu, 3. redimitus Diademate, 4. ten ens Sceptrum, 5. manu, stipatus frequently Aulicorum. Inter hos primarii sunt CancellariuSy 6. cum Consiliariis & Secretariis, Pmfectus PrcBtorii, 7. Aulce. M agister, 8. Pocillator (pincerna), 9. Dapifer, 10. Thesaurarius, 11. A re hiCubicularius, 1 2 . & Stabuli M agister, 1 3 .

Subordinantur his Nobiles Aulici, 14. Nobile Famulitium, 15. cum Cubiculariis, & Cursoribus, 16. Stipatores, 17. cum Satellitio.

Solemniter rccipit Legatos exterorum, 18.

Ablegat Vicarios suos, , dministra tores, PrcBfectos, Qucestores, & Legatos, aliorsum, quibus mittit Mandata nova subinde per Veredarios,, 19.

Morio, 20. movet Risum ludicris Actionibus.

The Soldier. - CXXXIX. – Miles.

If we be to make War *Soldiers* are lifted, 1.

Their *Arms* are a *Head-piece,* 2. (which is adorned with a *Crest*) and the *Armour,* whose parts are a *Collar,* 3. a *Breast-plate,* 4. *Arm-pieces,* 5. *Leg-pieces,* 6. *Greaves,* 7. with a *Coat of Mail,* 8. and a *Buckler,* 9. these are the defensive Arms. The offensive are a *Sword,* 10. a *two-edged Sword,* 11. a *Falchion,* 12. which are put up into a *Scabbard,* 13, and are girded with a *Girdle,* 14. or *Belt,* 15. (a *Scarf,* 16. serveth for ornament) a *two-handed Sword,* 17 and a *Dagger,* 18. In these is the *Haft,* with the *Pummel,* 20. and the *Blade,* 21. having a *Point,* 22. in the middle are the *Back,* 23. and the *Edge,* 24.

The other Weapons are a *Pike,* 25. a *Halbert,* 26. (in which is the *Haft,* 27. and the *Head,* 28.) a *Club,* 2,, and a *Whirlebat,* 30.

They fight at a distance with *Muskets,* 31. and *Pistols,* 32. which are charged with *Bullets,* 33. out of a *Bullet-bag,* 34. and with *Gun-powder* out of a *Bandalier,* 35.

Si bellandum est scribuntur *Milites.* 1.

Horum *Arma* sunt, *Galea* (Cassis, 2.) (quae ornatur *Cristâ*) & *Armatura,* cujus partes *Torquis ferreus,* 3. *Thorax,* 4. *Brachialia,* 5. *Ocreae ferreae,* 6. *Manicae,* 7. cum *Lorica,* 8. & *Scuto,* (Clypeo), 9. haec sunt Arma defensiva.

Offensiva sunt *Gladius,* 10, *Framea,* 11. & *Acinaces,* 12. qui reconduntur *Vaginâ,* 13. accinguntur *Cingulo,* 14. vel *Baltheo,* 15. (*Fascia militaris,* 16. inservit ornatui) *Romphaea,* 17. & *Pugio,* 18. In his est *Manubrium,* 19. cum *Pomo,* 20. & *Verutum,* 21. *Cuspidatum,* 22. in medio *Dorsum,* 23. & *Acies,* 24.

Reliqua arma sunt *Hasta,* 25. *Bipennis,* 26. (in quibus *Hastile,* 27. & *Mucro,* 28.) *Clava,* 29. & *Coestus,* 30.

Pugnatur eminiis *Bombardis* (Sclopetis), 31. & *Sclopis,* 32. quae onerantur *Globis,* 33. è *Theca bombardica,* 34. & *Pulvere nitrato* è *Pyxide pulveraria,* 35.

The Camps. - CXL. Castra.

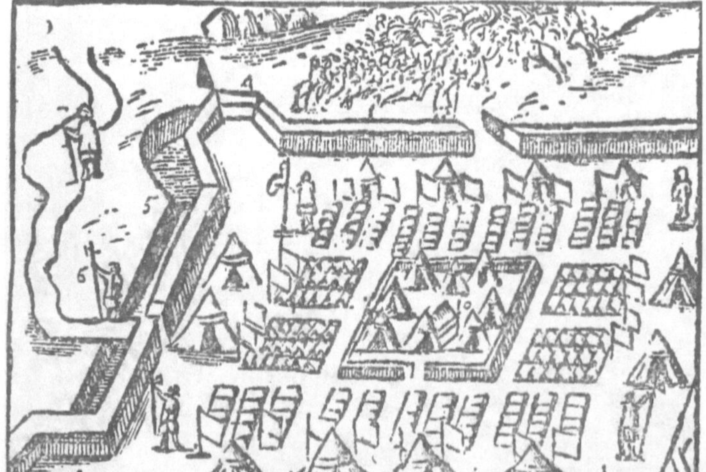

When a *Design* is undertaken the *Camp,* 1. is pitched and the *Tents* of *Canvas,* 2. or *Straw,* 3. are fastned with *Stakes;* and they entrench them about for security's sake, with *Bulwarks,* 4. and *Ditches,* 5. *Sentinels,* 6. are also set; and *Scouts,* 7. are sent out.

Sallyings out, 8. are made for Forage and Plunder-sake, where they often cope with the *Enemy,* 9. in skirmishing.

The *Pavilion* of the *Lord General* is in the midst of the *Camp,* 10.

Expeditione susceptâ, *Castra,* 1. locantur & *Tentoria Lintels,* 2. vel *Stramentis,* 3. figuntur *Paxillis;* eaque circumdant, securitatis gratiâ *Aggeribus,* 4. & *Fossis,* 5. *Excubiae,* 6. constituuntur; & *Exploratores,* 7. emittuntur.

Excursiones, 8. fiunt Pabulationis & Praedae causâ, ubi saepius confligitur cum *Hostibus,* 9. velitando.

Tentorium summi Imperatoris est in medio *Castrorum,* 10.

The Army and the Fight. - CXLI. - Acies & Praelium.

When the *Battel* is to be fought the *Army* is set in order, and divided into the *Front,* 1. the *Rere,* 2. and the *Wings,* 3.

The *Foot,* 4. are intermixed with the *Horse,* 5.

That is divided into *Companies,* this into *Troops.*

These carry *Banners,* 6. those *Flags,* 7. in the midst of them.

Their Officers are, *Corporals, Ensigns, Lieutenants, Captains,* 8. *Commanders of the Horse,* 9. *Lieutenant Colonels, Colonels,* and he that is the chief of all, the *General.*

The *Drummers,* 10. and the *Drumslades,* 11. as also the *Trumpeters,* 12. call to Arms, and inflame the Soldier.

At the first Onset the *Muskets,* 13. and *Ordnance,* 14. are shot off.

Afterwards they fight, 15. hand to hand with *Pikes* and *Swords.*

They that are overcome are slain, 16. or taken prisoners, or *run away,* 17.

They that are for the Reserve, 18. come upon them out of their *places where. they lay in wait.*

The *Carriages,* 19. are plundered.

Quando *Pugna* committenda est, *Acies* instruitur, & dividitur in *Frontem,* 1. *Tergum,* 2. & *Alas* (*Cornua*), 3.

Peditatus, 4. intermiscetur *Equitatui,* 5.

Ille distinguitur in *Centurias,* hic in *Turmas.*

Illae in medio ferunt *Vexilla,* 6. hae *Labara,* 7.

Eorum Praefecti sunt, *Decuriones, Signiferi, Vicarii, Centuriones,* 8. *Magistri Equitum,* 9. *Tribuni, Chiliarchae,* & summus omnium *Imperator.*

Tympanistae, 10. & *Tympanotribae,* 11. ut & *Tubicines,* 12. vocant ad Arma & inflammant Militem.

Primo Conflictu, Bombardae, 13. & *Tormenta,* 14. exploduntur.

Postea pugnatur, 15. cominus *Hastis* & *Gladiis.*

Victi trucidantur, 16. vel capiuntur, vel *aufugiunt,* 17.

Succenturiati, 18. superveniunt ex *insidiis.*

Impedimenta, 19. spoliantur.

The Sea-Fight. – CXLII. - Pugna Navalis.

A *Sea-fight* is terrible, when huge *Ships,* like *Castles,* run one upon another with their *Beaks,* 1. or shatter one another with their *Ordnance,* 2. and so being bored thorow they drink in their own Destruction, and are *sunk,* 3.

Or when they are set on fire and either by the firing of *Gun-powder,* 4. men are blown up into the air, or are burnt in the midst of the waters, or else leaping into the Sea are drowned.

A *Ship* that flieth away, 5. is overtaken by those that *pursue her,* 6. and is taken.

Navale proelium terribile est, quum ingentes *Naves,* veluti *Arces,* concurrunt Rostris, 1. aut se invicem quassant *Tormentis,* 2. atque ita perforatae, imbibunt perniciem suam & *submerguntur,* 3.

Aut quum igne corripiuntur, & vel ex incendio pulveris *tormentarii,* 4. homines ejiciuntur in aerem, vel exuruntur in mediis aquis, vel etiam desilientes in mare, suffocantur.

Navis fugitiva, 5. intercipitur ab *insequentibus,* 6. & capitur.

The Besieging of a City. - CXLIII. Obsidium Urbis.

A *City* that is like to endure a *Siege,* is first summoned by a *Trumpeter,* 1. and persuaded to *yield.* Which if it refuseth to do, it is assaulted by the Besiegers, and taken by storm.

Either by climbing over the walls with *Scaling-ladders,* 2. or breaking them down with *Battering-engins,* 3. or demolishing them with *great Guns,* 4. or breaking through the Gates with a *Petarr,* 5. or casting *Granadoes,* 6. out of *Mortar-pieces,* 7. into the City, by *Engineers,* 8. (who lye behind *Leagure baskets,* 9.) or overthrowing it with *Mines* by *Pioneers,* 10.

They that are besieged defend themselves from the *Walls,* 11. with fire and stones, &c, or *break out by force,* 12.

A *City that is taken by Storm* is plundered, destroyed, and sometimes laid even with the ground.

Urbs passura *Obsidionem,* primum provocatur per *Tubicinem,* 1. & invitatur ad *Depitionem.* Quod si abnuat facere, oppugnatur ab Obsidentibus & occupatur.

Vel muros per *Scalas,* 2, transcendendo, aut diruendo *Arietibus,* 3. aut demoliendo *Tormentis,* 4. vel dirumpendo portas *Exostra,* 5. vel ejaculando *Globos Tormentarios,* 6. e *Mortariis* (*balistis*), 7. in Urbem per *Balistarios,* 8. (qui latitant post *Gerras,* 9.) vel subvertendo *Cuniculis* per *Fossores,* 10.

Obsessi defendunt se de *Muris,* 11. ignibus, lapidibus, &c. aut *erumpunt,* 12.

Urbs vi expugnata, diriditur, exciditur, interdum equatur solo.

Religion – CXLIV. - Religio.

Godliness, 1. the Queen of Vertues, *worshippeth God,* 4. devoutly, the Knowledge of God being drawn either from the *Book of Nature,* 2. (for the work commendeth the Work-master) or from the *Book of Scripture,* 3. she meditateth upon his Commandments contained in the *Decalogue,* 5. and treading Reason under foot, that *Barking Dog,* 6. she giveth *Faith,* 7. and assent to the Word of God, and *calleth* upon him, 8. as a Helper in adversity.

Divine Services are done in the *Church,* 9. in which are the *Quire,* 10. with the *Altar,* 11. the *Vestry,* 12. the *Pulpit,* 13. *Seats,* 14. *Galleries,* 15. and a *Font,* 16. All men perceive that there is a God, but all men do not rightly know God.

Hence are divers *Religions* whereof IV. are reckoned vet as the chief.

Pietas, 1. Regina Virtutum *colit Deum,* 4. humiliter, Notitiâ Dei, haustâ vel ex *Libro Naturae,* 2. (nam opus commendat Artificem) vel ex *Libro Scripturae,* 3. recolit Mandata ejus comprehensa in *Decalogo,* 5. & conculcans Rationem, *oblatrantem Canem,* 6. praebet *Fidem,* 7. & assensum Verbo Dei, eumque *invocat,* 8. ut Opitulatorem in adversis.

Officia Divina fiunt in *Templo,* 9. in quo est *Penetrale* (Adytum, 10.) cum *Altari,* 11. *Sacrarium,* 12. *Suggestus,* 13. *Subsellia,* 14. *Ambones,* 15. & *Baptisterium,* 16.

Omnes homines sentiunt esse Deum, sed non omnes rectè nôrunt Deum. Hinc diversae *Religiones* quarum IV. numerantur adhuc primariae.

Gentilism. - CXLV. - Gentilimus.

The *Gentiles* feigned to themselves near upon XIIM. *Deities.*

The chief of them were *Jupiter,* 1. *President,* and *petty-God of Heaven; Neptune,* 2. of the Sea; *Pluto,* 3. of Hell; *Mars,* 4. of War; *Apollo,* 5. of Arts; *Mercury,* 6. of Thieves, Merchants, and Eloquence; *Vulcan,* (*Mulciber*) of Fire and Smiths; *Aeolus* of Winds: and the most obscene of all the rest, *Priapus.*

They had also Womanly Deities: such as were *Venus,* 7. the Goddess of Loves, and Pleasures, with her little son *Cupid,* 8. *Minerva* (*Pallas*), with the nine *Muses of Arts; Juno,* of Riches and Weddings; *Vesta,* of Chastity; *Ceres,* of Corn; *Diana,* of Hunting, and Fortune; and besides these *Morbona,* and *Febris* her self.

The *Egyptians,* instead of God worshipped all sorts of Beasts and Plants, and whatsoever they saw first in the morning.

The *Philistines* offered to *Moloch,* 9. their Children to be burnt alive,

The *Indians,* 10. even to this day, worship the *Devil,* 11.

Gentiles finxerunt sibi prope XIIM. *Numina.*

Eorum praecipua erant *Jupiter,* 1. *Praeses* & *Deaster coeli; Neptunus,* 2. Maris; *Pluto,* 3. Inferni; *Mars,* 4. Belli; *Apollo,* 5. Artium; *Mercurius,* 6. Furum, Mercatorum, & Eloquentiae; *Vulcanus* (*Mulciber*), Ignis & Fabrorum; *Aeolus,* V en to rum; & obscaenissimus, *Priapus.*

Habuerant etiam Muliebria Numina: qualia fuerunt *Venus,* 7. Dea Amorum, & Voluptatum, cum filiolo *Cupidine,* 8. *Minerva* (*Pallas*), cum novem *Musis*

Artium; Juno, Divitiarum & Nuptiarum; *Vesta,* Castitatis; *Ceres,* Frumentorum; *Diana,* Venationum; & Fortuna: quin & *Morbona,* ac *Febris* ipsa.

Aegyptii, pro Deo colebant omne genus Animalium & Plantarum, & quicquid conspiciebantur primum mane.

Philistaei offerebant *Molocho* (*Saturno*), 9. Infantes cremandos vivos.

Indi, 10. etiamnum venerantur *Cacodaemona,* 11.

Judaism. – CXLVI. - Judaismus.

Yet the true *Worship* of the true *God,* remained with the *Patriarchs,* who lived before and after the Flood.

Amongst these, that Seed of the Woman, the *Messias* of the World, was promised to *Abraham,* 1. the Founder of the *Jews,* the Father of them that believe: and he (being called away from the Gentiles) with his Posterity, being marked with the *Sacrament of Circumcision,* 2, made a peculiar people, and *Church* of God.

Afterwards God gave his *Law,* written with his own Finger in *Tables of Stone,* 5. to this people by *Moses,* 3. in Mount *Sinai,* 4.

Furthermore, he ordained the eating the *Paschal Lamb,* 6. and *Sacrifices* to be offered upon an *Altar,* 7. by *Priests,* 8. and *Incense,* 9. and commanded a *Tabernacle,* 10. with the Ark of the Covenant, 11. to be made: and besides, a *brazen Serpent,* 12, to be set up against the biting of Serpents in the Wilderness.

All which things were *Types* of the *Messias* to come, whom the *Jews* yet look for.

Verus tamem *Cultus* veri *Dei,* remansitapud *Patriarchas,* qui vixerunt ante & post Diluvium.

Inter hos. Semen illud Mulieris, *Messias* Mundi, promissus est *Abrahamo,* 1. Conditori *Judaeorum,* Patri credentium: & ipse (avocatus a Gentilibus) cum Posteris, notatus *Sacramento Circumcisionis,* 2. constitutus singularis populus, & *Ecclesia* Dei.

Postea Deus exhibuit *Legem* suam, scriptam Digito suo in *Tabulis Lapideis,* 5. huic Populo per *Mosen,* 3. in Monte *Sinai,* 4.

Porrò ordinavit manducationem *Agni Paschalis,* 6. & *Sacrificia* offerenda in *Altari,* 7. per *Sacerdotes,* 8. & *Suffitus,* 9. & jussit *Tabernaculum,* 10. cum Arca Foederis, 11. fieri: praeterea, *aeneum Serpentem,* 12. erigi contra morsum Serpentum in Deserto.

Quae omnia *Typi* erant *Messiae* venturi, quem *Judaei* adhuc expectant.

Christianity. - CXLVII. - Christianismus.

The only begotten eternal *Son of God,* 3. being promised to *our first Parents in Paradise,* at the last being conceived by the *Holy Ghost,* in the most Holy Womb of the *Virgin Mary,* 1. of the royal house of *David* and clad with humane flesh, came into the World at *Bethlehem* of *Judaea,* in the extream poverty of a *Stable,* 2. in the fullness of time, *in the year of the world* 3970, but pure from all sin, and the name of *Jesus* was given him, which signifieth a *Saviour.* When he was sprinkled with *holy Baptism,* 4. (the *Sacrament* of the *new Covenant*) by *John* his Forerunner, 5. in *Jordan,* the most sacred *Mystery* of the divine *Trinity,* appear'd by the *Father's* voice, 6. (whereby he testified that this was his *Son*) and the *Holy Ghost* in the shape of a *Dove,* 7. coming down from Heaven.

From that time, being the 30th year of his Age, unto the fourth year, he declared who he was, his words and works manifesting his Divinity, being neither owned, nor entertained by the *Jews,* because of his voluntary poverty. He was at last taken by these (when he had first instituted the *Mystical Supper,* 8, *of his Body and Blood* for a Seal of the *new Covenant* and the remembrance of himself) carried to the *Judgment-seat of Pilate,* Governour under *Caesar,* accused and condemned as an innocent *Lamb;* and being fastned upon a *Cross,* 9. *he dyed,* being sacrificed upon the Altar for the sins of the World.

But when he had revived by his Divine Power, he rose again the third day out of the *Grave,* 10. and forty days after being taken up from *Mount Olivet,* 11. into *Heaven,* 12. and returning thither whence he came, he vanished as it were, while the *Apostles,* 13. gazed upon him, to whom he sent his *Holy Spirit,* 14. from *Heaven,* the tenth day after his *Ascension,* and them, (being filled with his power) into the World to preach of him; being henceforth to come again to the *last Judgment,* sitting in the mean time *at the right hand of the Father,* and interceding for us.

From this *Christ* we are called *Christians,* and are saved in him alone.

Unigenitus aetenus *Dei Filius,* 3. promissus *Protoplastis in Paradiso,* tandem conceptus per *Sanctum Spiritum* in sanctissimo utero *Virginis Mariae,* 1. de domo regiâ *Davidis,* & indutus humanâ carne, prodiit in mundum *Bethlehemae Judaeâ,* in summâ paupertate *Stabuli,* 2. impleto tempore, *Anno Mundi* 3970, sed mundus ab omni peccato & nomen *Jesu* impositum fuit ei, quod significat *Salvatorem.* Hic. cum imbueretur *sacro Baptismo,* 4. (*Sacramento novi Foederis*) à *Johanne,* praecursore suo, 5. in *Jordane* apparuit sacratissimum *Mysterium* Divinae *Trinitatis, Patris* voce, 6. (quâ testabatur hunc esse *Filium* suum) & *Spiritu sancto* in specie *Columbae,* 7. delabente coelitus.

Ab eo tempore, tricesimo anno aetatis suae, usque an annum quartum, declaravit quis esset, verbis & operibus prae se ferentibus Divinitatem, nec agnitus, nec acceptus a *Judaeis,* ob voluntariam pauperatem.

Captus tandem ab his (quum prius instituisset *Coenam Mysticam,* 8. *Corporis & Sanguinis sui,* in Sigillum *novi Foederis,* & sui recordationem) raptus ad *Tribunal Pilati,* Praefecti *Caesarei,* accusatus & damnatus est *Agnus* innocentissimus; actusque in *Crucem,* 9. *mortem subiit,* immolatus in arâ pro peccatis mundi.

Sed quum revixisset Divinâ suâ Virtute, resurrexit tertia die è *Sepulchro,* 10. & post dies XL. sublatus de *Monte Oliveti,* 11. in *Coelum,* 12. & eo rediens unde venerat, quasi evanuit, *Apostolis,* 13. aspectantibus, quibus misit *Spiritum Sanctum,* 14. de *Coelo,* decima die post *Ascensum,* ipsos vero, (hac virtute impletos) in Mundum praedicaturos; olim rediturus ad *Judicium extremum,* interea sedens ad *dextram Patris,* & intercedens pro nobis.

Ab hoc *Christo* dicimur *Christiani,* inque eo solo salvamur.

Mahometism. - CXLVIII. - Mahometismus.

Mahomet, 1. a warlike Man, invented to himself a new Religion, mixed with *Judaism, Christianity* and *Gentilism,* by the advice of a *Jew,* 2. and an *Arian Monk,* 3. named *Sergius;* feigning, whilst he had the *Fit of the Falling-sickness,* that the *Archangel Gabriel* and the *Holy Ghost,* talked with him using a *Pigeon,* 4. to fetch Meat out of his Ear.

His *Followers* refrain themselves from *Wine;* are circumcised, have many *Wives;* build *Chapels,* 5. from the *Steeples* whereof, they are called to Holy Service not by *Bells,* but by a *Priest,* 6. they wash themselves often, 7. they deny the *Holy Trinity:* they *honour Christ,* not as the *Son of God,* but as a great *Prophet,* yet less than *Mahomet;* they call their *Law,* the *Alchoran.*

Mahomet, 1. Homo bellator, excogitabat sibi novam Religionem, mixtam ex *Judaismo, Christianismo* & *Gentilismo,* consilio *Judaei,* 2. & *Monachi Ariani,* 3. nomine *Sergii;* fingens, dum laboraret *Epilepsia.*

Archangelum Gabrielem, & *Spiritum Sanctum,* secum colloqui, adsuefaciens *Columbam,* 4. petere Escam ex Aure sua. *Asseclae* ejus abstinent se à *Vino;* circumciduntur, sunt *Polygami;* exstruunt *Sacella,* 5. de quorum *Turriculis,* convocantur ad sacra non a *Campanis,* sed a *Sacerdote,* 6. saepius se abluunt, 7. negant *SS. Trinitatem: Christum honorant,* non ut *Dei Filium,* sed ut magnum *Prophetam,* minorem tamen *Mahomete; Legem* suam vocant *Alcoran.*

Gods Providence. - CXLIX. - Providentia Dei.

Mens States are not to be attributed to *Fortune* or *Chance,* or the *Influence of the Stars,* (*Comets,* 1. indeed are wont to portend no good) but to the provident *Eye of God,* 2. and to his *governing Hand,* 3. even our *Sights,* or *Oversights,* or even our *Faults.*

God hath his *Ministers* and *Angels,* 4. who accompany a *Man,* 5. from his birth, as *Guardians,* against wicked *Spirits,* or the *Devil,* 6. who every minute iayeth wait for him, to tempt and vex him.

Wo to the mad *Wizzards* and *Witches* who give themselves to the *Devil,* (being inclosed in a *Circle,* 7. calling upon him with Charms) they dally with him, and fall from God! for they shall receive their reward with him.

Humanae Sortes non tribuendae sunt *Fortunae* aut *Casui,* aut *Influxui Siderum,* (*Cometae,* 1. quidem solent nihil boni portendere) sed provido *Dei Oculo,* 2. & ejusdem *Manui rectrici,* 3. etiam nostrae *Prudentiae,* vel *Imprudentiae,* vel etiam *Noxae.*

Deus habet *Ministros* suos, & *Angelos,* 4. qui associant se *Homini,* 5. à nativitate ejus, ut *Custodes,* contra malignos *Spiritus,* seu *Diabolum,* 6. qui minutatim struit insidias ei, ad tentandum vel vexandum.

Vae dementibus *Magis* & *Lamiis* qui Cacodaemoni se dedunt

(inclusi *Circulo,* 7. eum advocantes Incantamentis) cum eo colludunt & à Deo deficiunt! nam cum illo mercedem accipient.

The Last Judgment. - CL. - Judicium extremum.

For the *last day* shall come which shall raise up the Dead. 2. with the sound of a *Trumpet,* 1. and summon the *Quick* with them to the *Judgment-seat* of *Christ Jesus,* 3. (appearing in the Clouds) to give an Account of all things done.

When the *Godly* & *Elect,* 4. shall enter into life eternal into the place of Bliss, and the new *Hierusalem,* 5.

But the *Wicked* and the *damned,* 6. shall be thrust into *Hell,* 8. with the *Devils,* 7. to be there tormented for ever.

Nam *dies novissima* veniet, quae resuscitabit *Mortuos,* 2. voce *Tubae,* 1. & citabit *Vivos,* cum illis ad *Tribunal Jesu Christi,* 3. (apparentis in Nubibus) ad reddendam rationem omnium actorum.

Ubi *pii* (*justi*) & *Electi,* 4. introibunt in vitam seternam,in locum Beatitudinis & novum *Hierosolymam,* 5.

Impii vero. & *damnati,* 6. cum *Cacodaemonibus,* 7. in *Gehennum,* 8. detrudentur, ibi cruciandi seternum.

The Close - CLI. - Clausula.

Thus thou hast seen in short, all things that can be shewed, and hast learned the *chief Words* of the *English* and *Latin Tongue.*

Go on now and read other good *Books* diligently, and thou shalt become *learned, wise,* and *godly.*

Remember these things; fear God, and call upon him, that he may bestow upon thee the *Spirit of Wisdom*.

Farewell.

Ita vidisti summatim res omnes quae poterunt ostendi, & didicisti *Voces primarias Anglicae* & *Latinae Linguae.*

Perge nunc & lege diligenter alias bonos *Libros,* ut fias *doctus, sapiens,* & *pius.*

Memento horum; Deum time, & invoca eum, ut largiatur tibi *Spiritum Sapientiae.*

Vale.

www.ingramcontent.com/pod-product-compliance
Lightning Source LLC
LaVergne TN
LVHW101321110826
845152LV00011B/28

* 9 7 8 1 7 8 9 8 7 3 9 4 8 *